THORNTON WILDER

Other titles in the Greenhaven Press Literary Companion Series:

American Authors

Maya Angelou
Stephen Crane
Emily Dickinson
William Faulkner
F. Scott Fitzgerald
Nathaniel Hawthorne
Ernest Hemingway
Herman Melville
Arthur Miller
Eugene O'Neill
Edgar Allan Poe
John Steinbeck
Mark Twain

British Authors

Jane Austen
Charles Dickens
Joseph Conrad

World Authors

Fyodor Dostoyevsky
Homer
Sophocles

American Literature

The Adventures of
    Huckleberry Finn
The Catcher in the Rye
The Glass Menagerie
The Great Gatsby
Of Mice and Men
The Scarlet Letter

British Literature

Animal Farm
Beowulf
The Canterbury Tales
Lord of the Flies
Romeo and Juliet
Shakespeare: The Comedies
Shakespeare: The Histories
Shakespeare: The Sonnets
Shakespeare: The Tragedies
A Tale of Two Cities

World Literature

The Diary of a Young Girl

THE GREENHAVEN PRESS
Literary Companion
TO AMERICAN AUTHORS

READINGS ON

THORNTON WILDER

David Bender, *Publisher*

Bruno Leone, *Executive Editor*

Brenda Stalcup, *Managing Editor*

Bonnie Szumski, *Series Editor*

Katie de Koster, *Book Editor*

Greenhaven Press, San Diego, CA

Every effort has been made to trace the owners of copy-righted material. The articles in this volume may have been edited for content, length, and/or reading level. The titles have been changed to enhance the editorial purpose of the Opposing Viewpoints® concept. Those interested in locating the original source will find the complete citation on the first page of each article.

Library of Congress Cataloging-in-Publication Data

Readings on Thornton Wilder / Katie de Koster, book editor.
        p.   cm. — (The Greenhaven Press literary
    companion to American authors)
    Includes bibliographical references and index.
    ISBN 1-56510-815-9 (lib. : alk. paper). —
ISBN 1-56510-814-0 (pbk. : alk. paper)
    1. Wilder, Thornton, 1897–1975—Criticism and
interpretation. I. De Koster, Katie, 1948–   . II. Series.
PS3545.I345Z86   1998
818'.5209—dc21   98-9891
                                                            CIP

Cover photo: Archive Photos

Copyright ©1998 by Greenhaven Press, Inc.
PO Box 289009
San Diego, CA 92198-9009
Printed in the U.S.A.

> **EMILY:** . . . *Do any human beings realize life while they live it?—every, every minute?* **STAGE MANAGER:** *No. (Pause.) The saints and poets, maybe—they do some.*

—— Thornton Wilder, *Our Town*

Contents

wrote about social groups. Wilder was concerned with individuals, yet he found universal patterns in human experience that could be illustrated in the lives of people of any place or time.

Chapter 3: Pulitzer #1: *The Bridge of San Luis Rey*

Chapter 4: Pulitzer #2: *Our Town*

Chapter 5: Pulitzer #3: *The Skin of Our Teeth*

and presents a more satisfying conjunction of everyday
American life and universal issues.

FOREWORD

> *"'Tis the good reader that*
> *makes the good book."*
>
> Ralph Waldo Emerson

The story's bare facts are simple: The captain, an old and scarred seafarer, walks with a peg leg made of whale ivory. He relentlessly drives his crew to hunt the world's oceans for the great white whale that crippled him. After a long search, the ship encounters the whale and a fierce battle ensues. Finally the captain drives his harpoon into the whale, but the harpoon line catches the captain about the neck and drags him to his death.

A simple story, a straightforward plot—yet, since the 1851 publication of Herman Melville's *Moby-Dick*, readers and critics have found many meanings in the struggle between Captain Ahab and the whale. To some, the novel is a cautionary tale that depicts how Ahab's obsession with revenge leads to his insanity and death. Others believe that the whale represents the unknowable secrets of the universe and that Ahab is a tragic hero who dares to challenge fate by attempting to discover this knowledge. Perhaps Melville intended Ahab as a criticism of Americans' tendency to become involved in well-intentioned but irrational causes. Or did Melville model Ahab after himself, letting his fictional character express his anger at what he perceived as a cruel and distant god?

Although literary critics disagree over the meaning of *Moby-Dick*, readers do not need to choose one particular interpretation in order to gain an understanding of Melville's novel. Instead, by examining various analyses, they can gain numerous insights into the issues that lie under the surface of the basic plot. Studying the writings of literary critics can also aid readers in making their own assessments of *Moby-Dick* and other literary works and in developing analytical thinking skills.

The Greenhaven Literary Companion Series was created with these goals in mind. Designed for young adults, this unique anthology series provides an engaging and comprehensive introduction to literary analysis and criticism. The essays included in the Literary Companion Series are chosen for their accessibility to a young adult audience and are expertly edited in consideration of both the reading and comprehension levels of this audience. In addition, each essay is introduced by a concise summation that presents the contributing writer's main themes and insights. Every anthology in the Literary Companion Series contains a varied selection of critical essays that cover a wide time span and express diverse views. Wherever possible, primary sources are represented through excerpts from authors' notebooks, letters, and journals and through contemporary criticism.

Each title in the Literary Companion Series pays careful consideration to the historical context of the particular author or literary work. In-depth biographies and detailed chronologies reveal important aspects of authors' lives and emphasize the historical events and social milieu that influenced their writings. To facilitate further research, every anthology includes primary and secondary source bibliographies of articles and/or books selected for their suitability for young adults. These engaging features make the Greenhaven Literary Companion series ideal for introducing students to literary analysis in the classroom or as a library resource for young adults researching the world's great authors and literature.

Exceptional in its focus on young adults, the Greenhaven Literary Companion Series strives to present literary criticism in a compelling and accessible format. Every title in the series is intended to spark readers' interest in leading American and world authors, to help them broaden their understanding of literature, and to encourage them to formulate their own analyses of the literary works that they read. It is the editors' hope that young adult readers will find these anthologies to be true companions in their study of literature.

INTRODUCTION

One major biography of Thornton Wilder is called *The Enthusiast*, emphasizing that enthusiasm and an abiding belief in the ability of humankind to endure any calamity are hallmarks of Wilder's writing.

A popular teacher—he considered teaching his "real" vocation—Wilder loved finding novel ways to help his students learn. Enthusiasm and the ability to share knowledge and understanding by using seemingly simple examples were two of the characteristics that made him a favorite of his students. In teaching, as in writing and talking with friends, he drew on vast reserves of knowledge he eagerly gathered throughout his life. Theatrical director Tyrone Guthrie recalled a conversational style that matched the way he wrote:

> Wilder is learned but no pedant. I have never met anyone with so encyclopedic a knowledge of so wide a range of topics. Yet he carries this learning lightly and imparts it—the important with the trivial, the commonplace with the exceedingly bizarre—in a style and with a gusto which is all his own.

A good teacher eventually leads people to think and figure things out for themselves, while providing clues and guidance. Many of Wilder's works—and especially the three for which he won Pulitzer Prizes—explore and ultimately lead to an understanding of the common ground of humanity. He described his two Pulitzer-winning plays, *Our Town* and *The Skin of Our Teeth*, as viewing the same basic story from opposite ends of the telescope: The intimate, personal stories of the former echo the mythic sorrows, troubles, and joys of everyday living of the Antrobus family—the long-lived Adam, Eve, and entourage—in the latter.

Looking back over Thornton Wilder's work shortly before his death, the *New York Times* commented on the enduring popularity of his work:

Wilder's plays are now more than ever in rhythm with our changing habit of theatergoing. . . . He relates the moment to eternity, seeks the infinite in the immediate, finds the universe in each grain of wheat. His plays have not so much been "revived" over and over again, as they have almost continuously stayed alive among us.

THORNTON WILDER: A STUDY IN CONTRASTS

Edith J.R. Isaacs, editor of *Theatre Arts* magazine, remembers meeting Thornton Wilder in 1921 when Wilder was twenty-four years old. An aspiring playwright, he had just come from a postcollege year in Italy and France and was on his way to his first teaching job in New Jersey. Onboard the ship coming home he met theater reviewer Stark Young, who introduced him to Isaacs. After commenting on Wilder's having already "seen more of the world than many men ever see," Isaacs gives this picture of Wilder:

> It may have been something about the touch of many lands that gave him the double, but not at all divided, quality that is one of his distinguishing characteristics. Even in that first visit it was easy to see that although he was extremely serious, he was also very gay. Although very shy, he was unusually friendly; although he was surprisingly learned, he was never pedantic; he was as deliberate in his thinking as he was explosive in his speech, letting the words roll off his tongue one on top of the other but every one the right word aimed exactly at expressing the right idea. He was both temperate and enthusiastic, bold and unafraid but very modest, and above all he was one of the most amusing young men I had ever met.

This unassuming young man who went on to win three Pulitzer Prizes—unprecedentedly in two categories, fiction and drama—presented a series of contrasts in both his life and his work. An indifferent scholar, he was a voracious reader and an excellent teacher. He was a romantic at heart, but cast his works in classical form. His critical success was matched by popular acclaim; Bernard Grebanier, Brooklyn College professor emeritus of English, expressed the prevailing sense of surprise when he wrote: "Despite the three Pulitzer prizes awarded him Thornton Wilder may very well turn out to be one of the few enduring writers of our time."

Amos and Isabella Wilder

The contrasts in Thornton's life began with his parents, Amos and Isabella Wilder.

Amos Parker Wilder, son of a dentist who later founded a successful oilcloth manufacturing company, was raised in Augusta, Maine. He reported in the 1884 *Yale Class History* that during the after-school hours, "I was 'all over the place' . . . peddled things, carried water for elephants, worked in a grocery, and especially in a bookstore at odd hours." He was a bright and self-assured child, but when he entered the larger world of Yale University, his self-confidence suffered; "I was in terror of being dropped," he remembered later. Nonetheless, he was class orator in his first and second years, and Wilder biographer Linda Simon recounts some of his other academic and social successes:

> He was a member of Kappa Sigma Epsilon, Psi Upsilon, Skull and Bones; he sang in the class and university glee clubs, edited the *Courant* in his senior year, and acted as one of the class historians. His greatest disappointment—an embarrassment he was never to forget—came during his freshman year. He was selected for the staff of the *Record*, but was quickly dismissed for incompetency. "This was the severest humiliation I have ever known," he wrote later. In his small room on High Street he felt deeply dejected; but, characteristically, he summoned his strengths and rallied.

The humiliation may have spurred him to prove himself capable, for he later turned to the pen to make his living. After graduation, he taught school in Connecticut and Minnesota for a couple of years before taking a job as a reporter in Philadelphia. He then returned to New Haven for four years to earn a doctorate at Yale (his thesis was on municipal government) while editing the New Haven *Palladium.* He reveled in writing strongly opinionated editorials, one of which finally caused such controversy that he moved on to New York, where he worked for several papers. "Salaried journalism" did not have the job security he sought, though, so he bought a one-fourth interest in a Milwaukee, Wisconsin, newspaper, the *State Journal,* and became the paper's editor. Always one to keep busy, he also began giving a series of lectures on city government, sponsored by the University of Wisconsin.

In 1894 Amos married Isabella Thornton Niven, daughter of a Presbyterian minister from Dobbs Ferry, New York. The Wilders settled in Madison, Wisconsin, where their first son, Amos Niven, was born in 1895.

Isabella "was unlike her husband in temperament," notes Linda Simon:

> While Amos was outgoing, forceful, a fiery speaker, his wife was quiet and reserved. Though she had not been highly educated, she was artistic and refined. At Sunday school in her father's church, the teacher had found her "brilliant and highly cultivated." She had had aspirations of attending college or becoming a teacher, but her father, the Reverend Thornton Mac-Ness Niven, had definite restrictions for the education of his daughter. . . . Amos, too, showed a skepticism of Isabella's artistic inclinations. He was ever the patriarch and, for his wife and some of his children, a formidable force to confront.

Deterred from achieving her own ambitions (she had wanted to become a physician, but her father forbade it even after she had been accepted by Barnard College), Isabella Wilder did not abandon her aesthetic interests. Despite having four children in five years, Simon notes, "Neighbors would often see her taking her children on afternoon outings: her oldest son, Amos, was barely walking, steadying himself by holding on to the baby carriage with the three younger children inside, and Isabella herself would be pushing the carriage as she read a book of poetry."

THE MISSING TWIN

Those four children had nearly been five: On April 17, 1897, Isabella Wilder bore identical twins, but one son lived only a few hours. The surviving twin was named Thornton Niven, for Isabella's father. Born prematurely and weak, he had to be coddled for weeks to insure his survival. Perhaps this less-than-hale-and-hearty start predisposed his father to think of him as unable to care for himself; Amos Wilder more than once mourned that this "poor boy" would always be a burden.

Surviving his twin affected Thornton throughout his life. When he was twenty, he wrote his father, "I suppose that everyone feels that his nature cries out hourly for it knows not what, but I like to believe that mine raises an exceedingly great voice because I am a twin, and because by his death an outlet for my affection was closed." In later years, his older brother, Amos, wrote:

> Though Thornton and I were not twins, I have always felt that there was some sort of occult affinity in my makeup for his fabulations, like the telepathic understanding between Manuel and Esteban in *The Bridge of San Luis Rey*. . . . As himself a twin who lost a brother at birth, he was predisposed

to fascination with this relationship. Indeed one could hazard that he was haunted all his life by this missing alter ego. Thus he plays with the afterlife of this twin in the dual *persona* suggested by the title of his last novel, *Theophilus North*, "North," of course, representing an anagram for Thornton. In this was he was able to tease both himself and the reader as to the borderlands between autobiography and fable.

Observers also labeled as "his missing twin" Thornton's sister Isabel, who in later years handled his business and personal affairs and served as his intermediary with the public when he disappeared to write. These characterizations point up the closeness the children maintained throughout their lives, nurtured in part by their father's insistence that they write thoughtful letters to one another during their many separations.

Those first few years, though, brought few separations. From spring to fall the family (which now included Charlotte Elizabeth, born August 28, 1898, and Isabel, born January 13, 1900) lived in a rustic cottage on Lake Mendota, four miles from Madison. Thornton, now called Todger, was no longer frail, and "all the Wilders were lively; indolence was as alien as luxury," writes Thornton biographer Gilbert A. Harrison.

"Their intellectual growth was overseen by both parents," Simon notes, "with each contributing something in accordance with his or her personality. Amos preferred Scott, Dickens, and Shakespeare; Isabella, Yeats and Maeterlinck. Amos was concerned with imparting moral lessons; Isabella, a sense of beauty."

A LARGER ARENA

By the turn of the century, the outspoken Amos Parker Wilder, who now held a controlling interest in the *State Journal,* had become an important force in state politics. This had not led to financial security, though; a ratings war between newspapers and Wilder's crusade against corruption and alcohol (he refused to run liquor ads) cut sharply into the Wilders' income, making it ever harder to support his growing family. Yet beyond financial considerations, it was a desire to find a larger stage for his talents and a larger audience for his strong views that led Amos Wilder to seek a political appointment. A friend from Yale, William Howard Taft (who would later be elected president), was the secretary of war in President Theodore Roosevelt's cabinet. After

Amos was passed over for his first choice, as U.S. minister to Uruguay-Paraguay, he called on Taft to support his appointment as consul general at Hong Kong. He was confirmed in the post on March 7, 1906, and on May 7 the family landed in Hong Kong.

Thornton was enrolled in a strict, German-language school in Hong Kong. He remembered being carried about in a sedan chair and coming home for lunch with Wong, the "number one boy." But Isabella was unhappy in the colony, and on October 30 the rest of the Wilder clan left Amos behind and returned to the United States, settling in Berkeley, California. Here Thornton—with his mother's help—found the theater. His sister Isabel recalled Berkeley in her 1977 foreword to Thornton's play *The Alcestiad:*

> The magnificent Greek theater built into the hillside of a eucalyptus grove was a new and lively part of the life of the university and the town. Several times a year the Classics Department mounted productions of plays by Sophocles, Aeschylus, and Euripides. Our mother joined the volunteer workers in the costume shop and stenciled furlongs of borders in the Greek key or laurel leaf patterns on gorgeously colored togas. She made a little blue one with shells around the hem for Thornton—and a green one for brother Amos—and sent them off to apply for roles as members of the Athenean mob. Thus Thornton discovered "total" theater and the Golden Age of Antiquity. His experience until then had been a performance of *As You Like It* seen from the top gallery of a Milwaukee theater.
>
> By now Thornton was ten; black-haired, blue-eyed, acquisitive and radiant. Even before this he had claimed his share of a writer's allotment of the twenty-six letters of the alphabet and had begun to tame them into a vocabulary that would allow him—in good time—to speak in his own way. He went to bed early and got up early to write, and the full range of his enlarging vocabulary was turned to inventing dialogue. He draped us and the neighbors' children in yards of begged or borrowed cheesecloth and coaxed us into declaiming his grandiloquent speeches.

In 1909, after Amos took the post of consul general in Shanghai, he made two trips to California to be with his family. (A third daughter, Janet, was born in 1910.) He was nearly a stranger to his children. When he returned to Shanghai, his frequent letters exhorted his offspring to follow his own stern precepts. He frowned upon the Greek theater ("As for Greek plays, you know Papa has only a limited admiration for 'art.' . . . *Character* is the thing in life to strive for"), and instructed the children to read aloud to one another *Pilgrim's Progress, The Vicar of Wakefield,* and *The Boy's Life of John Wesley.*

Although the family enjoyed Berkeley, money was tight. Consuls general were instructed to help U.S. firms establish overseas business. The positions paid a modest salary and required a fair amount of entertaining; it was assumed that the companies they helped would be generous in helping them cover their expenses. Amos Wilder, ever sternly righteous, would never accept such remuneration. (He also refused to help companies that sold alcohol, even when instructed to do so by the State Department; he offered instead his resignation, which was not accepted.) The money Amos sent to Berkeley ($1,500 of his $8,000 salary) did not go far to support his wife and five children, and after the birth of Janet, the strain led most of the family (the younger Amos remained in California) to reunite in China once again.

Charlotte and Thornton were sent to the China Inland Mission Boys and Girls School at Chefoo, in Shantung Province. They were there, 450 miles north of Shanghai, when Sun-Yat Sen led a revolution in central China and was proclaimed president of the new republic. The turmoil does not seem to have affected their schooling, although Thornton wrote to his mother that the revolutionary army had offered the school's servants twice their salary to enlist. "Result: boys work; result: Wilder washes dishes and cleans carrots, serves table and carries water for other people (boys) to wash in (not himself! Oh no!)."

Discipline at the school was strict and the academic requirements were tough, especially since his schooling in Berkeley had not prepared him with the competence that was expected in Greek, Latin, algebra, and geometry. He and Charlotte were allowed a few minutes together once a week. Gilbert Harrison reports that "uniformed in white pith helmets and white suits with knee-length pants, the boys were marched on Sundays through hot, dusty streets to attend Church of England services, seeing on all sides goiters, tumors, abscesses, stumps of lepers' arms and legs, the blind, the skeletal Chinese children. It was Thornton's first sight of omnipresent misery—untended, ignored, endured." That recognition of the endurance of the human race would form the basis of some of his most powerful works.

Once again, Mrs. Wilder was unhappy living with her husband in China; this time she took the two younger daughters, Isabel and Janet, to stay with her sister in Florence, Italy. Charlotte and Thornton stayed at Chefoo, their brother Amos was still in Berkeley, and their father was in Shanghai.

Thornton had persuaded the school authorities to let him substitute long-distance running for the required group sports of soccer and cricket. His father deplored his failure to be a sportsman—not realizing until some years later that his second son was severely nearsighted—but Thornton exulted in the long stretches of time alone: He knew that writers needed such time, and he used his running time for thinking.

Students were required to write their parents every Sunday, so Thornton had to write both to Shanghai and to Florence. His letters to his father rarely had trouble conforming to the school's standards (they were read by a teacher before they were sent), but his fanciful letters to his mother occasionally elicited the comment, "Too fantastic!"

A year later, Mrs. Wilder, Isabel, and Janet returned to the United States, while Thornton, Charlotte, and Mr. Wilder sailed for California from China. (Mr. Wilder had contracted a debilitating tropical disease, Asian sprue, that left him listless and unhappy. He had resigned his post, and would never regain the vigorous health he had enjoyed before.) Thornton joined Amos at the Thacher School in the Ojai valley in California, a school that normally attracted affluent students. The headmaster, Sherman Thacher, was another Yale buddy of Thornton's father's, and with his help the boys were able to get an education they could not otherwise easily afford. In *Thornton Wilder: An Intimate Portrait,* Richard Goldstone notes that Amos warned his old friend about his younger son:

> He had "nerves," was "silent, sensitive," and slept badly; he could swim, but beyond that had no interest in sports; his interests, rather, were directed toward "music, art, drama and literature"; he was "not a good mixer," but was sensitive and self-conscious, though "radiantly happy when with those who like and understand him." Amos added, in relaying these unfortunate characteristics to Headmaster Thacher, that "he may develope 'moods'."

It was about this time that their father demanded a pledge of temperance from Thornton and Charlotte; he made them sign a promise never to drink alcohol. In Thornton's case, that promise did not take; by his college years, he was regularly enjoying social drinking. (Years later, Richard Goldstone asked him, "One of your most celebrated colleagues said recently that all a writer really needs is a place to work, tobacco, some food, and good whisky. Could you explain to the non-drinkers among us how liquor helps things along?" Wilder replied, "My springboard has always been long walks. I drink a great deal, but I do not associate it with writing.")

In his foreword to *The Angel That Troubled the Water and Other Plays,* Thornton remembered himself at sixteen:

> It is a discouraging business to be an author at sixteen years of age. Such an author is all aspiration and no fulfillment. He is drunk on an imaginary kinship with the writers he most admires, and yet his poor overblotted notebooks show nothing to prove to others, or to himself, that the claim is justified. The shortest walk in the country is sufficient to start in his mind the theme, the plan, and the title, especially the title, of a long book; and the shortest hour when he has returned to his desk is sufficient to deflate his ambition. . . .

> Authors of fifteen and sixteen years of age spend their time drawing up title pages and adjusting the tables of contents of works they have neither the perseverance nor the ability to execute. They compass easily all the parts of a book that are inessential. They compose dignified prefaces, discover happy quotations from the Latin and French, and turn graceful dedications.

That short attention span might have hampered a lesser writer, but Thornton kept writing a series of "three-minute plays for three persons." He went on to compose at least forty of these short works, finding in them "a literary form that satisfied my passion for compression" and avoided "the needless repetition, the complacency in most writing."

COLLEGE

After a year at Thacher, Thornton transferred to Berkeley High School, which Charlotte was attending, for two years, planning to attend his father's alma mater, Yale, when he graduated. But Amos Wilder feared Yale was too worldly for his spiritually inadequate son. Instead he enrolled Thornton in Ohio's Oberlin College, an evangelical college founded by two Congregational ministers, which Thornton's brother also attended. After two years, Amos was allowed to transfer to Yale, and Thornton wrote a friend that "I have [my father's] promise in writing for one year only." In the end, he spent two years at Oberlin, transferring to Yale under protest.

Although Amos had hoped Oberlin would mold his son into his own image, the Ohio campus held other interests for

Thornton. Among its many appeals, the school offered an excellent music department, an outlet for his passion for theater, and the "salons" of Mrs. Martin, the wife of one of the professors. Martin invited a circle of students to meet on Sunday afternoons. These salons were, writes Richard Goldstone, "of considerable importance to the young man's development of poise and self-assurance; there he could talk about theater, about new writers—George Moore was one of his enthusiasms—and he was respectfully listened to." He joined the editorial board of the *Literary Magazine* and was made archivist of the CYMOC club, a group of students that met monthly for intellectual discourse. (The members swore not to reveal what the initials CYMOC stood for.)

Besides the respect of his peers, Thornton was encouraged by Professor Charles H.A. Wager, the chairman of the English Department. Wager, whom Wilder described as "the greatest class lecturer I have ever heard," invited the young author home, "and encouraged him to read aloud the stories and plays which, a year or so before, he could show only to his mother," according to Goldstone.

So by the time Amos decided to transfer his younger son to Yale in New Haven (where the family was now established), Thornton was "completely devoted to Oberlin and deeply resented my father's moving me to the East." His father insisted, for several reasons: to bring the family together, to save money, and to earn a Yale diploma, which would be most valuable in finding a job in teaching, the profession he had decided on for Thornton.

During the summers, Amos required his sons to work at physical labor; he usually found a farm where they would be required to do chores in return for a small wage. Thornton also had one other break in his college career, from September 18 to December 31, 1918, when he joined the Coast Artillery Corps. He had long wanted to serve in the war being fought in Europe, World War I, but his nearsightedness had made him ineligible until just before the war ended. He resumed his studies in January 1919 and received his diploma in June 1920, listing his profession in the yearbook as journalist.

Not Exactly the Grand Tour

Thornton wanted to make his living as a writer; Amos thought that absurd. Richard Goldstone describes the father's worries:

Now fifty-six years old, his earning potential limited by age and dwindling opportunities, Amos, the head of a household consisting of four females and an elder son about to enter the ministry, saw in Thornton the only bulwark—and an insubstantial one at that—against poverty and disgrace should he, Amos, be stricken and incapacitated. Not for a moment did Amos entertain the thought that Thornton could, through writing, maintain even himself ("Carving olive pits!" "Carving olive pits!"). Viewing his second son as basically ineffectual, somewhat indolent, and not overly intelligent, Amos reached the conclusion that Thornton could eke out a living in the only way open to failures and incompetents: as a schoolmaster. Having arrived at that decision through his own inexorable logic, Amos communicated it to Thornton who, faced with the vision of his mother and sisters facing starvation, bowed to Necessity and accepted his Lot.

But first there would be a brief respite. Thornton would be allowed to spend a year as a resident visitor at the American Academy in Rome. He could learn Italian and brush up on his Latin—both useful for a teacher—while performing some healthy physical labor swinging a pickax at the school's archeological digs. Why Italy? His mother had discovered that the exchange rate for dollars was at that time very favorable. After due consideration, Gilbert Harrison reports, Amos told his son:

> My dear boy, . . . I am going to give you $900, in installments. If the money situation over there is as your mother says it is, that will sustain you very well for a year. . . . So make the most of your advantages in Rome. When you return, I hope you will be prepared to teach Latin in some school somewhere, and as far as money is concerned, let me not hear another word out of you for the rest of our lives.

Although the more immediate product of Thornton's Italian journey was his first novel, *The Cabala*, part of the influence of this year abroad later found its way into Wilder's *Our Town*. In a preface for that play, he wrote:

> For a while in Rome I lived among archeologists, and ever since I find myself occasionally looking at the things about me as an archeologist will look at them a thousand years hence. Rockefeller Center will be reconstructed in imagination from the ruins of its foundations. How high was it? A thesis will be written on the bronze plates found in New York's detritus heaps—"Tradesmen's Entrance," "Night Bell."

> In Rome I was led through a study of the plumbing on the Palatine Hill. A friend of mine could ascribe a date, "within ten years," to every fragment of cement made in the Roman Republic and early Empire.

An archeologist's eyes combine the view of the telescope with the view of the microscope. He reconstructs the very distant with the help of the very small.

It was something of this method that I brought to a New Hampshire village.

LEARNING FRENCH

At the end of eight months, money running short, Thornton prepared to leave Italy. He had been hinting to his father that it would be a good idea for him to go to Paris (which was becoming a mecca to expatriate Americans, especially expatriate American writers), "to learn French." As one of the two positions Amos was contemplating for his son was as a teacher of French, he agreed to finance a few weeks in France but warned Thornton to return promptly, ready to teach the language at Lawrenceville, a New Jersey prep school. Lawrenceville agreed to hire Thornton for $1,500 per year on the recommendations of his Yale professors, and Thornton wrote to his mother (then in England): "Well, well, I am as excited as a decapitated goose." He enjoyed Paris, but returned early to New York to take French lessons at the Berlitz School.

MADE TO BE A TEACHER

Unexpectedly, Thornton enjoyed his new job, which included housemaster duties for the thirty-two boys who lived at Davis House. Nights after ten, weekends, and vacations were devoted to writing; the rest of his hours were devoted to his students. Gilbert Harrison writes that he was a popular teacher:

> The boys were entertained by his rapid walk and talk and grateful for his cheerful tolerance of their nonsense. He was *different.* "Mr. Wilder seemed to find us endlessly intriguing and disturbing," one of the boys, Marshall Sprague, recalled, "though we knew that his interest was that of a spectator at the zoo watching the monkeys, charming and repulsive by turns, happy to be noticed, especially when he erupted like a volcano at some misconduct of ours and threw blackboard erasers and chalk at us." They retaliated by dropping a trunk down the stairs from the third floor, so that it would knock the door off his room and end up inside. . . .
>
> He tried without conspicuous results to introduce French into everyday conversation. For the enlightenment of one lad who was having trouble with irregular verbs, in this instance the present tense of venir, he leapt over the back of a couch, flapping his arms and shouting "On wings of gauze they come!

they come! ILS VIENNENT!'" . . . First-year boys were directed in scenes from a popular Broadway show, *Nelly Kelley,* taught to sing "Don't Send Me Roses When It's Shoes That I Need" and how to form a chorus line. Halfway through the study period, Mr. Wilder visited all rooms to observe work habits, decisively solving such problems as a snake crawling between sheets. At bed-check, he rushed to a window and shouted, "No, madam! You can't come in. This is a boy's room!" Yes, Mr. Wilder was *different.*

Thornton supplemented his salary with other small jobs: preparing a publisher's catalog and tutoring during the school year, more tutoring during summer breaks, and finally publication of a portion of the book he was working on, then called *Memoirs,* in a small New Orleans magazine, *Double Dealer.* He finally had enough money to send some to his family and offer, "Tell me when you need more."

THE PARENTAL INFLUENCE

Amos Wilder, who would die in 1935, no longer controlled his son's life. While biographers and critics uniformly agree that Isabella Wilder nurtured, supported, and encouraged her son's gifts, they disagree on the influence of Thornton's father.

At least one biographer, Richard Goldstone, believes Amos Wilder's influence on his second son was harmful. He notes that Isabella was unlike most American women, who stayed with their husbands in diplomatic postings and sent the children to boarding school:

> There is no avoiding what is more than a possibility that, in 1906, she effected the separation of her children from her husband because she had already observed that his influence was unwholesome and psychologically damaging. Not only did Amos's stern Calvinism hang like a cloud over the young children, but he imposed on them his iron will, his lofty standards of conduct, achievement, and principle, and his sense of himself—law-giver and dispenser of absolute justice. . . .

> Maintaining a fatherless household [in Berkeley] was to be a struggle—financial and physical—for Isabella. . . . But whatever the physical handicaps she encountered in making do with the meager allowance remitted by her husband, Isabella was enabled to remedy—if remedy she could—the psychologically crippling influence that her husband exerted upon their children.

Those who feel Amos was a hindrance rather than a brace to his talented son find support in such outbursts as Thornton's defense of himself and his oldest sister in this letter to his father, written when he was twenty-one:

Sometimes I get so annoyed by your desperation over a chance cigarette or a frivolous word that I have a good mind to give you a real jolt, such jolts as other fathers get from their sons, the real griefs of Old Eli [Yale]. I am too good for you, that's all, and you make a luxury of martyrdom to yourself out of my slightest defection. Likewise Charlotte's friends consider her an amazing, rare personality, such as New England is only able to cast up once in an age, but you wear us all out with your instigations to Napoleonship and fame [and] look upon the first YMCA secretary or Settlement House directress as more interesting than Charlotte. Do try to console and comfort your declining years with the incredible news that you have produced at least two children that are the amazement and delight and amused despair of their circles (the more finely grained the spectator the greater the appreciation). Let others produce obscure devoted women and faithful Assistant Pastors; you have fathered two wild fowl flying in the storm of the 20th century.

Thornton's brother offers a different perspective on biographers' speculations in *Thornton Wilder and His Public:*

It is inevitable that I should give special attention to the role of our father in my brother's development. . . . This parent of Maine background had certain of the robust and granitic traits and that "interfering spirit of righteousness" associated with the Calvinist heritage, a type widely derided today. My brother had his troubles with him. . . . But the paradox in this case was that this same overshadowing father was also the one who imbued my brother with his deepest insights into American grass-roots values and their hidden operations.

Although Thornton thought of his father as "a sort of Don Quixote" without any sense of the aesthetic, writes Gilbert Harrison,

Still, Thornton took from him a desire to shape and improve lives, a facility with language, a histrionic virtuousity, moral energy, nostalgia for small towns and respect for anonymous multitudes. . . .

However hard-pressed, he had always found the money a child needed. He had sent his son to farms not as punishment but to provide lessons in the value of the dollar and in health building. His strictures were not motivated by selfish concerns, certainly not by dislike. Whatever the frustrations of his married life, he held that "the drama of the home is a great mystery," a mystery Thornton would celebrate in his plays, and that nowhere else do all manner of men "grow tender and have longings to be good: hugging their children and walking about in the dark hours safeguarding their dependents." Moreover, Papa's conviction that literature would not pay was commonplace for his generation.

ROMAN MEMOIRS

At the end of the spring 1924 term, Thornton requested a two-year leave of absence from Lawrenceville, intending to finish his *Memoirs* and try to find a publisher. He spent that summer at the MacDowell Colony in Peterborough, New Hampshire, the first of several stays at the prestigious artists colony, where he was encouraged by the benefactor of the colony, Mrs. Edward Mac-Dowell, and managed to finish five of the portraits for *Memoirs*. At the end of that year, he submitted part of the manuscript to New York publishers Albert and Charles Boni. The Bonis were mildly encouraging and Wilder completed more sections; they finally offered him a contract in November 1925. By then Wilder had returned to school, attending Princeton to earn a master of arts degree in Romance languages. If the book—now called *The Cabala*—did not sell well, he counted on the M.A. to help him find better-paying work.

The book appeared in April 1926, and was hailed by the *New York Times* as "the debut of a new American stylist" and a "magnificent literary event." Other critics agreed, and sales were respectable. But when Thornton discovered that his contract said that no payment was due him until February 15, 1927, he realized he could not live on his earnings as an author just yet. He accepted a job as chaperone to Europe for a young man; he could travel and be paid for it, earning enough to last until Christmas. However, the young man, twenty-year-old Andy Townson, proved an uncongenial companion; by the time he left for home at the beginning of December 1926, Thornton was impatient to get back to work on his next book, *The Bridge of San Luis Rey*. He wrote his publisher and asked for $150 against his royalties so he could resume work on the book in Europe, now that he no longer had the Townson subsidy to cover his living expenses. He considered rooming with Ernest Hemingway to save money, but "his wife is about to divorce him and his new wife is about to arrive from America; so I think I better not try." He wrote, went to the Riviera for Christmas, dropped in on Sylvia Beach at her famous Paris bookstore Shakespeare and Company, and wrote his mother that he was homesick. At the end of January 1927 he sailed for home.

THE BRIDGE OF SAN LUIS REY

Occasional tutoring jobs to meet expenses continued to eat away at his writing time; when Lawrenceville invited him to return as master of Davis House, he agreed to come for one school year, 1927–1928. Perhaps the anticipation of a secure position helped; within two weeks of accepting the position, he finally finished the manuscript he had been working on, *The Bridge of San Luis Rey.* Ironically, when the book came out that fall, Thornton was recuperating from surgery for appendicitis and anxious to return to Lawrenceville; "otherwise, what will become of my SALARY."

The book was a smash hit. By December, it had earned him $20,000 in royalties—quite a sum for a man who was eager to return to a $4,000-a-year position as a schoolteacher. The excitement—especially after the book was awarded the 1928 Pulitzer Prize for fiction—made teaching school difficult. But it did bring a measure of celebrity that had him hobnobbing with the famous: Gene Tunney, world heavyweight boxing champion, invited him to dinner (the two men, who got on well, would later go on a walking tour in Europe together). Broadway producer Jed Harris asked for the right of first refusal on Thornton's next play. And Scott and Zelda Fitzgerald invited him to spend a weekend with them at the house they had rented in Delaware.

SUCCESS

Thornton could do what he wanted now, without worrying overmuch about money. His mother had long wanted the family to have a house of their own; he purchased property in Hamden, Connecticut, in March 1929 and spent a substantial part of his new earnings on "The House *The Bridge* Built." With Thornton's help, his father, who was physically ailing, retired from working and spent much of the next few years in sanitoriums or on health farms. Besides supporting his parents, he also provided for Isabel (and, after the mid-1930s, for Charlotte); only Amos and Janet—the oldest and youngest siblings—were making their own way. Isabel began to take over the day-to-day work Thornton's celebrity necessitated; she dealt with his mail, acted as literary agent, served as hostess, dealt with the myriad details that did not interest Thornton. He never married, and this convenient arrangement continued until he died. Isabel often traveled with Thornton; besides running interference in practical matters, she was a congenial sounding board for his new ideas.

He was working on *The Woman of Andros* when the stock market collapsed at the end of October 1929, marking what would become known as the Great Depression. When the book was finally published, it did not seem appropriate or "socially relevant" during a period of widespread hardship; critics were especially hard on its foreign setting, and a vitriolic attack by proletarian writer Michael Gold in the *New Republic,* entitled "Wilder: Prophet of the Genteel Christ," lambasted him for not having written a novel about the working class. His next book, *Heaven's My Destination,* was a sympathetic and funny picture of middle America.

CHICAGO

Thornton still loved teaching, and had happily accepted a position at the University of Chicago for the appealing sum of $666.66 per month. He later said that his years in Chicago, 1930–1936, were the happiest of his life. He became a member of a group of men and women who were bright without being intellectual, fun loving and informal. The longtime loner ecstatically told his friend Alexander Woollcott, the *New Yorker*'s theater critic, "They love me humanly and I love them inhumanly."

Despite his new affluence, Wilder did not spend money easily on himself. "Things don't speak to me," he noted with dismay when people showered him with presents. Two suits would suffice for summer, and when he gained weight, Isabel could let them out so he could get another five years' wear out of them. He provided for his family, contributed to a wide variety of charities, and took pleasure in treating his friends generously.

In 1934 Gertrude Stein came from France to give a series of lectures on English literature; she had not returned to her native country for over three decades. Wilder invited Stein and her companion, Alice B. Toklas, to stay in his apartment while they were in Chicago. She and Wilder struck up a friendship that lasted until her death in 1946; during the years to come she would often importune him to collaborate with her on her next book. He always graciously avoided the requests, but tirelessly championed her writing and wrote introductions for three of her books.

BACK TO THE THEATER

In 1939 *The Bridge of San Luis Rey* was one of the first ten Pocket Books—twenty-five-cent paperbacks—published in the United States. But regardless of the enduring popularity of the novel, Malcolm Goldstein, author of *The Art of Thornton Wilder*, chronicles his subject's return to his early love, the theater:

> After the publication of *Heaven's My Destination* Wilder made up his mind to write no more fiction. The decision did not come as a result of the poor showing of the novel, he later insisted, but from a growing dissatisfaction with narrative technique: he had become uncomfortably conscious of his "editorial presence." By this he meant the prodding and emphasizing of theme from an all-seeing, all-knowing position. . . . He turned to the form which at least seemed to prohibit a sense of the author's presence. In drama the author does not hover over the personalities of the characters, cannot point directly to those of their traits which express the meaning of the play, and is, in fact, expected to make his revelations through action and dialogue alone. Gertrude Stein had taught him that "you should talk to yourself in your own private language and be willing to sink or swim on the hope that your private language has nevertheless sufficient correspondence with that of persons of some reading and experience." From 1937 to 1943 in accordance with this principle he wrote and brought to Broadway *Our Town, The Merchant of Yonkers,* and *The Skin of Our Teeth.*

Two of those three plays won him Pulitzer Prizes for drama; Wilder saw them as basically the same story, seen through opposite ends of a telescope. The third, *The Merchant of Yonkers,* was a disappointment at the time. But when he rewrote it as *The Matchmaker* in 1954, it achieved immense popularity, as did the musical version, *Hello, Dolly!*

World War II had begun in 1939, and soon after the Japanese bombed Pearl Harbor in December 1941 Wilder chose to join the military; he was commissioned a captain in the air force. He had a few weeks before he had to report, so when Alfred Hitchcock asked for his help on the script for *The Shadow of a Doubt,* he traveled to Hollywood for intensive sessions with the great director. Hitchcock was so impressed with his work that he rode the train with him back to Washington, discussing the screenplay all the way. Wilder's own play *The Skin of Our Teeth* opened just before he was to go overseas; its message of the enduring strength of the human race was aimed at a wartime audience.

After the war, Wilder went back to work: teaching and lecturing, writing, even acting occasionally. He was especially popular as the Stage Manager in *Our Town,* and he also enjoyed playing Mr. Antrobus in *The Skin of Our Teeth.* In collaborating with Sol Lesser on the movie production of

Our Town, he agreed to give Emily a reprieve:

> In the first place, I think Emily should live. I've always thought so. In a movie you see people so *close to* that a different relation is established. In the theatre they are halfway abstractions in an allegory; in the movie they are very concrete. So, insofar as the play is a generalized allegory, she dies—we die—they die; insofar as it's a concrete happening it's not important that she die; it's even disproportionately cruel that she die.

> Let her live. The idea will have been imparted anyway.

His teaching assignments now were no longer the refuge of the inept or unsuccessful. Harvard awarded him the Charles Eliot Norton Professorship of Poetry; he lectured on Thoreau, Poe, Whitman, Dickinson, and Melville. Other honors followed, including the 1952 gold medal for fiction from the American Academy of Arts and Letters, the 1963 U.S. Presidential Medal of Freedom (the first year the award was given for distinguished civilian service in peacetime), and the 1968 National Book Award for *The Eighth Day.* He continued to write: *Theophilus North* was published in 1973. But he did not live to see the publication of the play he had been working on since before the Second World War, *The Alcestiad;* it was published posthumously in 1977.

On December 22, 1975, in its Transitions column, *Newsweek* magazine offered an obituary for Wilder, who had died on December 7; "Exit the Stage Manager" was written by Bill Roeder in the style of *Our Town.* It ended this way:

> He was getting up in years at the age of 78. Still, it was a jolt for us folks in Grover's Corners—and I'll bet for a whole lot of other people, too—when Thornton Wilder slipped away with a heart attack during his afternoon nap the other day. God rest him. H'm—11 o'clock in Grover's Corners. You get a good rest, too. Good night.

CHAPTER 1

A Personal Perspective on Wilder

An Interview with the Author

Richard H. Goldstone

In the late 1950s the *Paris Review* published a series of interviews with such prominent authors as William Faulkner, Georges Simenon, Truman Capote, and Thornton Wilder. Wilder was interviewed by Richard H. Goldstone, who would later write *Thornton Wilder: An Intimate Portrait* and coedit *Thornton Wilder: An Annotated Bibliography of Works by and about Thornton Wilder*. In the interview, Goldstone and Wilder discuss a wide variety of topics, including the author's need for daily contact with nonartists, the difference between novels and plays, and the social functions of drama.

It is unlikely that more than a few of his countless friends have seen Wilder in repose. Only then does one realize that he wears a mask. The mask is no figure of speech. It is his eyeglasses. As do most glasses, they partially conceal his eyes. They also distort his eyes so that they appear larger: friendly, benevolent, alive with curiosity and interest. Deliberately or not, he rarely removes his glasses in the presence of others. When he does remove them, unmasks himself, so to speak, the sight of his eyes is a shock. Unobscured, the eyes—cold light blue—reveal an intense severity and an almost forbidding intelligence. They do not call out a cheerful "Kinder! Kinder!"; rather, they specify: "I am listening to what you are saying. Be serious. Be precise."

Seeing Wilder unmasked is a sobering and tonic experience. For his eyes dissipate the atmosphere of indiscriminate amiability and humbug that collects around celebrated and gifted men; the eyes remind you that you are confronted by one of the toughest and most complicated minds in contemporary America.

An apartment overlooking the Hudson River in New York City. During the conversations, which took place on the evening of December 14, 1956, and the following afternoon, Mr. Wilder could watch the river lights or the river barges as he meditated his replies. . . .

INTERVIEWER: Although military service is a proud tradition among contemporary American writers, I wonder if you would care to comment on the circumstance that you volunteered in 1942, despite the fact that you were a veteran of the First World War. That is to say, do you believe that a seasoned and mature artist is justified in abandoning what he is particularly fitted to do for patriotic motives?

WILDER: I guess everyone speaks for himself in such things. I felt very strongly about it. I was already a rather old man, was fit only for staff work, but I certainly did it with conviction. I have always felt that both enlistments were valuable for a number of reasons.

One of the dangers of the American artist is that he finds himself almost exclusively thrown in with persons more or less in the arts. He lives among them, eats among them, quarrels with them, marries them. I have long felt that portraits of the non-artist in American literature reflect a pattern, because the artist . . . portrays the man in the street as he remembers him from childhood, or as he copies him out of other books. So one of the benefits of military service, *one* of them, is being thrown into daily contact with non-artists, something a young American writer should consciously seek—his acquaintance should include also those who have read only *Treasure Island* and have forgotten that. Since 1800 many central figures in narratives have been, like their authors, artists or quasi-artists. Can you name three heroes in earlier literature who partook of the artistic temperament?

INTERVIEWER: Did the young Thornton Wilder resemble George Brush, and in what ways?

WILDER: Very much so. I came from a very strict Calvinistic father, was brought up partly among the missionaries of China, and went to that splendid college at Oberlin at a time when the classrooms and student life carried a good deal of the pious didacticism which would now be called narrow Protestantism. And that book [*Heaven's My Destination*] is, as it were, an effort to come to terms with those influences.

The comic spirit is given to us in order that we may analyze, weigh, and clarify things in us which nettle us, or which we are outgrowing, or trying to reshape. That is a very autobiographical book.

INTERVIEWER: Why have you generally avoided contemporary settings in your work?

WILDER: I think you would find that the work is a gradual drawing near to the America I know. I began with the purely fantastic twentieth-century Rome (I did not frequent such circles there); then Peru, then Hellenistic Greece. I began, first with *Heaven's My Destination,* to approach the American scene. Already, in the one-act plays, I had become aware of how difficult it is to invest one's contemporary world with the same kind of imaginative life one has extended to those removed in time and place. But I always feel that the progression is there and visible; I can be seen collecting the practice, the experience and courage, to present my own times. . . .

A WRITER'S HISTORY

INTERVIEWER: I don't know exactly how to put the next question, because I realize you have a lot of theories about narration, about how a thing should be told—theories all related to the decline of the novel, and so on. But I wonder if you would say something about the problem of giving a "history" or a summary of your life in relation to your development as a writer.

WILDER: Let's try. The problem of telling you about my past life as a writer is like that of imaginative narration itself; it lies in the effort to employ the past tense in such a way that it does not rob those events of their character of having occurred in freedom. A great deal of writing and talking about the past is unacceptable. It freezes the historical in a determinism. Today's writer smugly passes his last judgment and confers on existing attitudes the lifeless aspect of plaster-cast statues in a museum. He recounts the past as though the characters knew what was going to happen next. . . .

INTERVIEWER: Did you have a happy childhood?

WILDER: I think I did, but I also think that that's a thing about which people tend to deceive themselves. Gertrude Stein once said, "Communists are people who fancied that they had an unhappy childhood." (I think she meant that the kind of person who can persuade himself that the world would be completely happy if everyone denied himself a vast number of free decisions, is the same kind of person who could persuade himself that in early life he had been thwarted and denied all free decision.) I think of myself as having been—right up to and through my college years—a sort of sleepwalker. I was not a dreamer, but a muser and a self-amuser. I have never been without a whole repertory of absorbing hobbies, curiosities, inquiries, interests. Hence, my head has always seemed to me to be like a brightly lighted room, full of the most delightful objects, or perhaps I should say, filled with tables on which are set up the most engrossing games. I have never been a collector, but the resource that I am describing must be much like that of a collector busying himself with his coins or minerals. Yet collectors are apt to be "avid" and competitive, while I have no ambition and no competitive sense. Gertrude also said, with her wonderful yes-saying laugh, "Oh, I wish I were a miser; being a miser must be so occupying." I have never been unoccupied. That's as near as I can get to a statement about the happiness or unhappiness of my childhood. Yet I am convinced that, except in a few extraordinary cases, one form or another of an unhappy childhood is essential to the formation of exceptional gifts. Perhaps I should have been a better man if I had had an unequivocally unhappy childhood.

INTERVIEWER: Can you see—or analyze, perhaps—tendencies in your early years which led you into writing?

WILDER: . . . The future author is one who discovers that language, the exploration and manipulation of the resources of language, will serve him in winning through to his way. This does not necessarily mean that he is highly articulate in persuading or cajoling or outsmarting his parents and companions, for this type of child is not usually of the "community" type—he is at one remove from the persons around him. (The future scientist is at eight removes.) Language for him is the instrument for digesting experience, for explaining himself to himself. Many great writers have been extraordinarily awkward in daily exchange, but the greatest give the impression that their style was nursed by the closest attention to colloquial speech. . . .

THE DRAMATIST'S PARADOX

INTERVIEWER: Well now, inasmuch as you have gone from story-telling to playwriting, would you say the same tendencies which produced the novelist produced the dramatist?

WILDER: I think so, but in stating them I find myself involved in a paradox. A dramatist is one who believes that the pure event, an action involving human beings, is more arresting than any comment that can be made upon it. On the stage it is always *now;* the personages are standing on that razor-edge, between the past and the future, which is the essential character of conscious being; the words are rising to their lips in immediate spontaneity. A novel is what *took place;* no self-effacement on the part of the narrator can hide the fact that we hear his voice recounting, recalling events that are past and over, and which he has selected— from uncountable others—to lay before us from his presiding intelligence. Even the most objective novels are cradled in the authors' emotions and the authors' assumptions about life and mind and the passions. Now the paradox lies not so much in the fact that you and I know that the dramatist equally has selected what he exhibits and what the characters will say—such an operation is inherent in any work of art—but that all the greatest dramatists, except the very greatest *one,* have precisely employed the stage to convey a moral or religious point of view concerning the action. The theater is supremely fitted to say: "Behold! These things are." Yet most dramatists employ it to say: "This moral truth can be learned from beholding this action."

The Greek tragic poets wrote for edification, admonition, and even for our political education. The comic tradition in the theater carries the intention of exposing folly and curbing excess. Only in Shakespeare are we free of hearing axes ground.

INTERVIEWER: How do you get around this difficulty?

WILDER: By what may be an impertinence on my part. By believing that the moralizing intention resided in the authors as a convention of their times—usually, a social convention so deeply buried in the author's mode of thinking that it seemed to him to be inseparable from creation. I reverse a popular judgment: we say that [George Bernard] Shaw wrote diverting plays to sugar-coat the pill of a social message. Of these other dramatists, I say they injected a didactic intention in order to justify to themselves and to their audiences the exhibition of pure experience.

INTERVIEWER: Is your implication, then, that drama should be art for art's sake?

WILDER: Experience for experience's sake—rather than

for moral improvement's sake. When we say that [Dutch painter Jan] Vermeer's *Girl Making Lace* is a work of art for art's sake, we are not saying anything contemptuous about it. I regard the theater as the greatest of all art forms, the most immediate way in which a human being can share with another the sense of what it is to be a human being. This supremacy of the theater derives from the fact that it is always "now" on the stage. It is enough that generations have been riveted by the sight of Clytemnestra luring Agamemnon to the fatal bath, and Oedipus searching out the truth which will ruin him; those circumambient tags about "Don't get prideful" and "Don't call anybody happy until he's dead" are incidental concomitants.

INTERVIEWER: Is it your contention that there is no place in the theater for didactic intentions?

WILDER: The theater is so vast and fascinating a realm that there is room in it for preachers and moralists and pamphleteers. As to the highest function of the theater, I rest my case with Shakespeare—*Twelfth Night* as well as *Macbeth.*

INTERVIEWER: If you will forgive me, I'm afraid I've lost track of something we were talking about a while back—we were talking about the tendencies in your childhood which went into the formation of a dramatist.

WILDER: The point I've been leading up to is that a dramatist is one who from his earliest years has found that sheer gazing at the shocks and countershocks among people is quite sufficiently engrossing without having to encase it in comment. It's a form of tact. It's a lack of presumption. That's why so many earnest people have been so exasperated by Shakespeare: they cannot isolate the passages wherein we hear him speaking in his own voice. Somewhere Shaw says that one page of Bunyan,[1] "who plants his standard on the forefront of—I-forget-what—is worth a hundred by such shifting opalescent men."

DRAMA'S SOCIAL FUNCTIONS

INTERVIEWER: Are we to infer from what you say that the drama ought to have no social function?

WILDER: Oh, yes—there are at least two. First, the presentation of *what is,* under the direction of those great hands, is important enough. We live in *what is,* but we find a thousand

1. seventeenth-century English preacher John Bunyan, author of *The Pilgrim's Progress*

ways not to face it. Great theater strengthens our faculty to face it.

Secondly, to be present at any work of man-made order and harmony and intellectual power—Vermeer's *Lace Maker* or a Haydn quartet or *Twelfth Night*—is to be confirmed and strengthened in our potentialities as man.

INTERVIEWER: I wonder if you don't hammer your point pretty hard because actually you have a considerable element of the didactic in you.

WILDER: Yes, of course. I've spent a large part of my life trying to sit on it, to keep it down. The pages and pages I've had to tear up! I think the struggle with it may have brought a certain kind of objectivity into my work. I've become accustomed to readers' taking widely different views of the intentions in my books and plays. A good example is George Brush, whom we were talking about before. George, the hero of a novel of mine which I wrote when I was nearly forty, is an earnest, humorless, moralizing, preachifying, interfering product of Bible-belt evangelism. I received many letters from writers of the George Brush mentality angrily denouncing me for making fun of sacred things, and a letter from the Mother Superior of a convent in Ohio saying that she regarded the book as an allegory of the stages in the spiritual life.

Many thank me for the "comfort" they found in the last act of *Our Town;* others tell me that it is a desolating picture of our limitation to "realize" life—almost too sad to endure.

Many assured me that *The Bridge of San Luis Rey* was a satisfying demonstration that all the accidents of life were overseen and harmonized in providence; and a society of atheists in New York wrote me that it was the most artful exposure of shallow optimisms since *Candide*[2] and asked me to address them.

A very intelligent woman to whom I offered the dedication of *The Skin of Our Teeth* refused it, saying that the play was so defeatist. ("Man goes stumbling, bumbling down the ages.") *The Happy Journey to Trenton and Camden* received its first performance, an admirable one, at the University of Chicago. Edna St. Vincent Millay happened to be in the audience. At the close of the play she congratulated me at having so well pictured that "detestable bossy kind of mother."

2. tale of the adventures of a determinedly optimistic young man by eighteenth-century French philosopher Voltaire

Most writers firmly guide their readers to "what they should think" about the characters and events. If an author refrains from intruding his point of view, readers will be nettled, but will project into the text their own assumptions and turns of mind. If the work has vitality, it will, however slightly, alter those assumptions.

INTERVIEWER: So that you have *not* eliminated all didactic intentions from your work after all?

WILDER: I suspect that all writers have some didactic intention. That starts the motor. Or let us say: many of the things we eat are cooked over a gas stove, but there is no taste of gas in the food. . . .

ONLY ONE OR TWO IDEAS

INTERVIEWER: Someone has said—one of your dramatist colleagues, I believe, I can't remember which one—that a writer deals with only one or two ideas throughout his work. Would you say your work reflects those one or two ideas?

WILDER: Yes, I think so. I have become aware of it myself only recently. Those ideas seem to have prompted my work before I realized it. Now, at my age, I am amused by the circumstance that what is now conscious with me was for a long time latent. One of those ideas is this: an unresting preoccupation with the surprise of the gulf between each tiny occasion of the daily life and the vast stretches of time and place in which every individual plays his role. By that I mean the absurdity of any single person's claim to the importance of his saying, "I love!" "I suffer!" when one thinks of the background of the billions who have lived and died, who are living and dying, and presumably will live and die.

This was particularly developed in me by the almost accidental chance that, having graduated from Yale in 1920, I was sent abroad to study archaeology at the American Academy in Rome. We even took field trips in those days and in a small way took part in diggings. Once you have swung a pickax that will reveal the curve of a street four thousand years covered over which was once an active, much-traveled highway, you are never quite the same again. You look at Times Square [in New York City] as a place about which you imagine some day scholars saying, "There appears to have been some kind of public center here."

This preoccupation came out in my work before I realized it. Even *Our Town,* which I now see is filled with it, was not so consciously directed by me at the time. At first glance, the play appears to be practically a genre study of a village in New Hampshire. On second glance, it appears to be a meditation about the difficulty of, as the play says, "realizing life while you live it." But buried back in the text, from the very commencement of the play, is a constant repetition of the words "hundreds," "thousands," "millions." It's as though the audience—no one has ever mentioned this to me, though—is looking at that town at ever greater distances through a telescope.

I'd like to cite some examples of this. Soon after the play begins, the Stage Manager calls upon the professor from the geology department of the state university, who says how many million years old the ground is they're on. And the Stage Manager talks about putting some objects and reading matter into the cornerstone of a new bank and covering it with a preservative so that it can be read a thousand years from now. Or as minister presiding at the wedding, the Stage Manager muses to himself about all the marriages that have ever taken place—"millions of 'em, millions of 'em . . . Who set out to live two by two . . ." Finally, among the seated dead, one of the dead says, "My son was a sailor and used to sit on the porch. And he says the light from that star took millions of years to arrive." There is still more of this. So that when finally the heartbreak of Emily's unsuccessful return to life again occurs, it is against the background of the almost frightening range of these things.

Then *The Skin of Our Teeth,* which takes five thousand years to go by, is really a way of trying to make sense out of the *multiplicity* of the human race and its affections.

So that I see myself making an effort to find the dignity in the trivial of our daily life, against those preposterous stretches which seem to rob it of any such dignity; and the validity of each individual's emotion.

INTERVIEWER: I feel that there is another important theme running through your work which has to do with the nature of love. For example, there are a number of aphorisms in *The Bridge of San Luis Rey* which are often quoted and which relate to that theme. Do your views on the nature of love change in your later works?

WILDER: My ideas have not greatly changed; but those aphorisms in *The Bridge* represent only one side of them and are limited by their application to what is passing in that novel. In *The Ides of March*, my ideas are more illustrated than stated.

Love started out as a concomitant of reproduction; it is what makes new life and then shelters it. It is therefore an affirmation about existence and a belief in value. Tens of thousands of years have gone by; more complicated forms of society and of consciousness have arisen. Love acquired a wide variety of secondary expressions. It got mixed up with a power conflict between male and female; it got cut off from its primary intention and took its place among the refinements of psychic life, and in the cult of pleasure; it expanded beyond the relations of the couple and the family and reappeared as philanthropy; it attached itself to man's ideas about the order of the universe and was attributed to the gods and God.

I always see beneath it, nevertheless, the urge that strives toward justifying life, harmonizing it—the source of energy on which life must draw in order to better itself. In *The Ides of March* I illustrate its educative power (Caesar toward Cleopatra and toward his wife; the actress toward Marc Antony) and its power to "crystallize" idealization in the lover (Catullus's infatuation for the destructive "drowning" Clodia—he divines in her the great qualities she once possessed). This attitude has so much the character of self-evidence for me that I am unable to weigh or even "hear" any objections to it. I don't know whether I am uttering an accepted platitude or a bit of naïve nonsense.

A Brother's Perspective

Amos Niven Wilder

"Though Thornton and I were not twins, I have always felt that there was some sort of occult affinity in my makeup for his fabulation, like the telepathic understanding between Manuel and Esteban in *The Bridge of San Luis Rey*," wrote Amos Wilder. In the following excerpt from his book *Thornton Wilder and His Public*, Amos—Thornton's elder brother by eighteen months—derides the critics who believe Thornton's work must be unimportant because it is popular. Although his brother's work is both accessible and appealing, he says, it has been distilled by a keen and discerning mind from an immense repertoire of material ranging from international literature (in many languages) and intellectual discussions and correspondence with brilliant thinkers to Wilder's own humanist convictions.

There is a greater analogy between the instinctive life of the wider public and the talent of a great writer . . . than in the superficial verbiage and the changing criteria of the official judges.[1]

—Marcel Proust

For some time the critics by and large have not been able to fit the novels and plays of Thornton Wilder into their picture of modern writing and its agenda. They evidently have some qualms about this, since his work was so innovative and versatile and has had so profound a resonance in a wide public both at home and abroad. Yet there is a certain traditionalism in his outlook which undermines the modern premise. In his best-known plays and in much of his fiction he appears to speak for a grass-roots American experience which they may look on as banal, insipid, or moralistic. But what if his "notation of the heart" is, indeed, that of Mr. and

1. *A la recherche du temps perdu* (Pléiade edn., vol. III). Paris, 1957. pp. 893–894.

Mrs. Antrobus, that is, Everyman? And what if his inquisition goes beneath the sentiment of Grover's Corners or the Philistinism of Coaltown, Illinois, to some deeper human marrow?

It is a question of the anonymous millions in our streets and countryside, and of finding a register and a language for their potential. In 1957 Wilder spoke on "Culture in a Democracy" to a German audience in Frankfurt at the award of the Peace Prize of the German publishers.[2] He took as his text a shocking passage from Walt Whitman: Is there one of the great classics of the ancients or of Europe "that is consistent with these United States . . . or whose underlying basis is not a denial and insult to democracy?" He went on to speak of the dangers but also of the "unknown factors" and the "promise" of an enfranchised society of equals of the kind which Whitman had envisaged. This kind of passionate empathy for Grover's Corners or Main Street—both magnanimous and austere—is too often missing in our modern classics and our critics of culture. The response to change and its advocacy takes precedence over the deeper human continuities.

CRITICAL SUSPICION OF POPULAR SUCCESS

Critics and critical schools in this country have understandably been suspicious of writers who have had large popular success. They have been baffled by any conjunction of true excellence with midbrow or lowbrow appeal as registered in the categories of "best-seller" or "book-club" selection. In the case of Wilder there has been a long history of embarrassment if not attack, and even of assignment to limbo. One can recall disparagement of the first three novels as effete or precious; [literary critic Richard] Blackmur's dissatisfaction with *Heaven's My Destination* as aimed at the book clubs; the critics' "snubbing" of *The Ides of March;* more recently, dismissal by Stanley Kauffmann and others of *The Eighth Day* as a sermon or an exercise in old clichés.

As for the plays, while they are continually being staged at the grass-roots level throughout the country, any more ambitious revival is likely to meet the critical incomprehension which recently greeted *The Skin of Our Teeth* in its Bicentennial presentation in New York.

2. *Kultur in einer Demokratie.* Frankfurt, 1957.

For awareness of this dilemma one can cite a review in the London *Times Literary Supplement* of Wilder's last novel, *Theophilus North.*

> In a literary career spanning half a century, Thornton Wilder has successfully resisted any kind of classification as novelist or playwright. We cannot pin him down, as we can Hemingway or Scott Fitzgerald, to background or subject matter (though both his first and his latest books are almost entirely autobiographical), and it is impossible to group him conveniently with any coterie of writers, whether prewar or postwar. Popularity and success—implicit in the huge sales (10,000 copies a week) of *The Bridge of San Luis Rey*—may have dented his reputation a little among those for whom starving in a garret is the sole criterion of artistic excellence. How, on the other hand, are we to account for the fact that in several European countries Mr. Wilder, along with Shakespeare and Joyce, is one of a mere handful of English-speaking writers known to the reading public?[5]

Yet many accomplished critics by now have their minds made up. Wilder, they agree, is indeed somewhat anomalous and hard to pigeonhole, but he falls outside the main line of advance of the novel or the drama. His work has been on the margin of those explorations and engagements so essential to our twentieth-century experience. Worst of all, he smacks of Middle America and even a disguised religiosity. Thus all across the board—subject matter, outlook, style—he does not fit the common premise or lend himself to the central debate.

In seeking to identify the reservations of the critics we can at least set aside some of the earlier imputations. Literary judges have long disallowed partisan Marxist charges made against him in the thirties, even if changing categories of social realism and relevance may still be invoked. *Our Town* is no longer banned in the USSR despite its alleged complaisance with the bourgeois family. *The Skin of Our Teeth* is similarly permitted there, though formerly excluded on the ground that wars and other calamities are not attributed in it to capitalist exploitation.

Critics have also now long dropped the charge of plagiarism against one of James Joyce's most revering excavators and glossators. Wilder happily conceded that, like some irreproachable predecessors, if he was a shoplifter he always preyed upon the best emporia. As Emerson remarks in his essay on Shakespeare, "Thought is the property of him who can entertain it and of him who can adequately place it."

THE BASIC PREMISE OF MODERN LETTERS

The reservations of the critics today have other grounds. Their disparagement, neglect, or bracketing of Wilder's work is not necessarily to be put down to the insensitivity of reviewers or to critical fashion and partisanship. The situation is much more interesting than that. As I have suggested, it comes down to the basic premise with regard to modern letters. One must beg the original question. Where, indeed, does the main engagement lie in our modern situation? Granted that "modernism" has had a great and necessary task of liberation to carry out in our epoch, what may have been left out in its view of that task and its engagement with our contemporary reality? . . .

The modern focus has understandably been one of revolt and emancipation, and Thornton Wilder has not been a stranger to it. But there should always be those who speak for the deeper ground which continues through change. Perhaps artists of this kind fall through the net of the existing tribunals. While the instinctive response of the wider public recognizes them, the official judges are at a loss.

When one moves the question to the American scene the issues become clearer. How do we define the "modern" here, and what is the relation of its proper iconoclasm to our older American heritage? It is a question of locating the deeper potential and the hidden springs of our many-layered society. One premise is that the clue and norm for us runs from the expatriates after World War I down through those writers who have extricated themselves not only from an earlier "genteel" tradition but from any rootage in what seem the blinkered pieties and conformisms of an older America.

It is true that many of our best writers have rightly been in revolt against Philistinism and inhumanity in our folkways. In aesthetic terms they have rightly sought a new language and new vehicles for a new sensibility. But, along with the critics, have they not also scanted the depths of our people and left a great deal of unfinished business? The fertility of the New World has always thrown up its own original and even plebeian celebrations, versions of its own native mythology. Here is one point at which Thornton Wilder comes in.

CRITICAL MYOPIA

Nothing is more revealing of critical myopia than assignment of Wilder to the category of "midcult." Granted that this is a step up from "masscult," it still connotes ingratiation of a Philistine public. But is the general public so obtuse and so negligible? This kind of classification makes things too easy for the critic. It is his task to distinguish between the wheat and the straw, and not only between the modern and the traditional. Just as there is a great deal of the new which is mainly imitative and of mediocre talent, so there is much of the seeming traditional which is highly creative in its own context and horizon. But the category of midcult sweeps both the saccharine and the profoundly disciplined into one common basket. One recalls how grudgingly many critics came to concede the merits of Robert Frost.

Even more shallow is the implied judgment on the wider public. There are in our population various kinds of literacy and illiteracy, various registers and acoustics for the arts and the imagination. No doubt there is much of the moronic, the sentimental, and the crass. These exhibit themselves also in many of our iconoclastic novelties. But the great continental public "out there," seemingly regressive and insensitive, is highly complex and unpredictable. No one dogma or program of the aesthetic should pretend to arbitrate for so rich and incalculable a gestation.

In any society, granted a wide mediocrity, if there is a valid pioneering elite of artists and intellectuals, there is also a diffused and unrecognized remnant which bears the heritage of the many and its costs and its promise. However scornful the elite may be of Main Street and suburbia, it should not cut itself off from the voices that witness through the shapeless and the inarticulate.

DISTILLING SIMPLICITY FROM A RICH BASE

In assigning Wilder to midcult, certain critics identify his work with cliché, banality, and indulgence. But this is to overlook certain highly rigorous aspects of his work. Such glossy or superficial writings as can properly be assigned to this category rest, for example, on no such extensive literacy as that of my brother, no such intimacy with the great models and their exacting demands. Whatever readability for a general public his books possess, this simplicity or wide appeal rests on an immense repertoire of aesthetic and intellectual tuition, which is, as it were, distilled in them. The ambiance of his thought, his mental climate or *habitus* was that of the masters, and there is no greater achievement of the "art of the difficult" than that of simplicity, if that is the word for it.

I can suggest the range of this American writer's acquaintance with the world of letters by offering a few examples. His familiarity with the Greek and Roman classics is evident in much of his writing. This goes back especially to the year he spent after his graduation from Yale at the American Academy in Rome. It was especially on classical epic and drama that he lectured during numerous summer terms at the University of Chicago. Classicists will appreciate the significance of the close friendship and animated conversation he carried on over a period with the great scholar Karl Reinhardt, discussions that bore not only on the Greek tragedians but also on such German poets as Hölderlin.

As for Romance languages his early stylistic "crush" on Mme. de Sévigné carried over, of course, to *The Bridge of San Luis Rey,* in which the letters of the Marquesa de Montemayor to her daughter echo the pattern. Thornton's M.A. degree at Princeton was in French under Professor Louis Cons, and his earliest teaching, at the Lawrenceville School, was in this department. Later, one of his longtime distractions, as a problem in literary detection, was the dating of the plays of the Spanish dramatist, Lope de Vega, a topic on which he wrote a paper for the Modern Language Association. He enjoyed his correspondence with the leading Spanish authority on this intricate topic, as he did his correspondence with Walter Lowrie about Kierkegaard, to whose work Lowrie had introduced him when they were both in Rome where the former was rector of the American church, St. Paul's.

Another picture-puzzle passion of Thornton's for years was his annotation of *Finnegans Wake,* the decoding of which inevitably required a large fund of linguistic and literary resource. In a quite different sector Thornton also followed with close attention the publication of the many volumes of the Yale Edition of *Horace Walpole's Correspondence,* edited by his friend and former schoolmate, Wilmarth Lewis. The latter has testified to the helpfulness of my brother's many letters about Walpole and the acuteness of his observations. They both had been introduced to the writers of this period by the great Chauncey Tinker at Yale.

I refer at a later point to Thornton's acquaintance with Goethe and other German writers and the opening this afforded him especially to circles of German students in his visits to that country. Other areas of literary initiation could be cited, not least the American classics on which he lectured at Harvard. Yet though he was in so many respects a polymath, in his own writing he availed himself of all such resources in his own sovereign way.

In categorizing his role as an American writer this broad literary culture should be kept in mind. It was this range of his literacy which explains the mutual cordiality and correspondence between him and Edmund Wilson. Both were "men of letters" in the European sense. With this kind of tuition Thornton's art, however accessible to a wide public, could never be popular in a disparaging sense. Nor should his academic associations be viewed as suspect since his humanism was as deep as it was wide.

PUTTING THE WORKS IN CONTEXT

Assessment of my brother's contribution in the long run will need to take account of more than his few novels and plays. Their resonance can be trivialized if seen out of context. In this case the author's life and work were interwoven, and one illuminates the other. There are writers best known for a few works who, nevertheless, constitute one kind of "presence" in their period, one kind of option or index or even synthesis in their times. Their writings can have a kind of divinatory impact related to the cultural scene, and this is related to their personal history and involvements. What Thornton Wilder represented in terms of cultural ripeness and mastery—as teacher, figure in world letters, correspondent, idea man and conversationalist—all this reflects itself in his formal writings, and vice versa. Just as in his plays, so in his quicksilver-like talk, whether at the Algonquin Hotel or in a PEN [International Association of Poets, Playwrights, Editors, Essayists, and Novelists] session abroad or a college common room or a bar, he brought worlds together and sparkled with searching insights.

Commentators have, indeed, been puzzled by the fact that he wrote so little and by those intervals in his career in which he did not seem to be productive. Even the wider public had heard of projects which he did not complete such as the Kafka-like play to be called *The Emporium* or the cycles of one-act plays devoted to the seven ages of man and to the seven deadly sins, both series evidencing his interest in modernizing the old "morality" genre typified by *Everyman*. It was suggested that he too easily allowed himself to be diverted by academic appointments or cultural missions, or even by war service.

It is true that he could joke about a proposed epitaph: "Here lies a man who tried to be obliging." Annals of his residence terms in Burton-Goodspeed Hall at the University of Chicago and in Harvard's Dunster House evoke the protracted meal times and midnight sorties with students, the fledgling manuscripts read, the many speaking appointments acccptcd, and the personal crises of youth for which he was so skillful and austere an analyst. There were wider calls he could not refuse: an unexpected additional course at Harvard; some Broadway production of a friend calling for a translation from the French, or requiring surgery; a plea from Alfred Hitchcock and Hollywood.

But this artist's role included all such gregariousness, involvement, pedagogy, and missions. His private fabulation carried over into all such public and oral occasions. His theater carried over into daily life. His formal works are related to this wider deportment as sage, mage, democrat, and soldier. He liked to act in his own plays. There was something of the histrionic in all he did. When he lectured he was all over the platform and down the aisles, gesturing, challenging, clowning, and taking the parts of the characters discussed. So it was also with his talk on more intimate occasions. His gusto and affections evoked scenarios "as good as a play."

LITERATURE IS A PART OF LIFE

With some authors, life is one thing and literature another. When this observation was made to Edmund Wilson he replied: "But isn't literature simply a part of life as much as conversation?" In the case of my brother, at least, this is highly pertinent. Like his conversation—understood either as his talk or in the old biblical sense of his deportment or way in the world—his novels and plays were gestures or overflow of his life. I cannot therefore deplore that he spent himself in so many other theaters at the expense of his writing.

In retrospect, what may well deserve attention in the cultural history of our period will be Wilder as a distinctive type and product of our American society. His formal works will only be part of the total image. No doubt other authors will be credited with greater achievement in their own kind. Other novelists and playwrights will be identified with crucial movements in the age. But at the level where American roots are linked with modern sophistication, and where American moralities are linked critically and imaginatively with old-world legacies, there have been fewer witnesses in our time. No doubt humanist scholars have sought to bridge these gaps. But what is more difficult, yet essential, is that these poles should be linked in art and poetry.

One test of this scope and role is afforded by international cultural encounters. On certain occasions when meetings were held abroad under such auspices as UNESCO [United Nations Educational, Scientific, and Cultural Organization] it was difficult to find American delegates who were not only scholars familiar with European literature past and present, but also and at the same time creative artists whose work was appreciated abroad. That Wilder could fill this double role and share in discussions in several languages meant a unique kind of American participation in Western culture. The same kind of total humanistic outreach was exhibited in the Goethe Festival at Aspen in 1949 when . . . my brother found himself called on to assist on the platform with the translation of the addresses of Albert Schweitzer on one day and of Ortega y Gasset on the next.

LARGE CHARITY AND UNCOMPROMISING SEVERITY

I have been illustrating my brother's extensive acquaintance with the world of letters as one answer to the charge of banality or indulgence in his writing. But rigor rather than indulgence appears also in the ethos of his work. If there is, indeed, a large charity in his portrayal of life and much gaiety, yet no one should miss the uncompromising severity that accompanies these. There was iron in his outlook, some combination perhaps of granite from Calvin and worldly wisdom from his cherished Goethe. We can recognize it not only in the austere Caesar of *The Ides of March* but also in the disabused acidity that runs through *The Skin of Our Teeth*. The unmasking of human motivation associated with modern thought was taken up by him into a more radical suspicion. But it did not leave him in the condition of so many who are tempted to cynicism, or who have nothing but pathos to fall back on with respect to their heroes or anti-heroes. This combination of generosity of spirit with austerity is far from sentimentality, but equally uncongenial to many moderns.

Even in the first year of his exposure to Europe and his ravishment by its high culture, when in Italy he was piecing together his most fastidious novel, *The Cabala* (at one time to be called *Romans*), he writes in a letter home: "A horror grows on me for the purely aesthetic; I am fierce for the strange, the strong, the remorseless; even the brutal and the coarse. The vivid and the significant; not the graceful.". . .

A MORE UNIVERSAL VISION

Thornton Wilder was no stranger to the anomie of our epoch. And just as he was intimate over long periods of immersion in the works of Kafka, Joyce, Proust, Broch, Stein, and other modern masters, so he was at home with the great pioneers and iconoclasts of modern thought and with the master texts and pamphlets of the time. Just as his earlier correspondence echoed his attention to Kierkegaard, Spengler, Lukács, and Valéry, so his later letters show him absorbed in the successive volumes of Lévi-Strauss. It should be clear from this review that he was no outsider to the cultural and aesthetic dislocations of our period or the great debates which have accompanied them. Whatever "Puritan" or "academic" or "classicist" liabilities may be charged against him and against his family background, these do not appear to have isolated him from the main currents of the age. Quite the converse, they may rather have endowed him with a deeper human orientation that could assimilate the new experience in a more universal vision.

CHAPTER 2

Major Themes in Thornton Wilder's Work

The Master of High Comedy

J.D. McClatchy

In this essay marking the one hundredth anniversary of the birth of Thornton Wilder, poet and critic J.D. McClatchy, editor of the *Yale Review*, deplores the "sophisticated" tendency to judge Wilder a sentimentalist and therefore no longer relevant. As a master of high comedy, rueful joy, and deep humanity, McClatchy maintains, Wilder should be ranked among such artists as Jane Austen and Ivan Turgenev.

A friend of mine, now a distinguished author and scholar, remembers that as a teen-ager in California she would wander in the stacks of the Berkeley Public Library. One day, with a random curiosity, she picked a novel off the shelf and turned to the opening paragraph. "The earth sighed as it turned in its course; the shadow of night crept gradually along the Mediterranean, and Asia was left in darkness. The great cliff that would one day be called Gibraltar held for a long time a gleam of red and orange . . . at the mouth of the Nile the water lay like a wet pavement." She was enthralled. She decided right there to become a writer, and hoped sometime, somehow to write sentences as ravishing as these. The novel was *The Woman of Andros*, by Thornton Wilder.

Others have had a similar experience with Wilder's books. Mine came later than my friend's, and therefore less dramatically, but the pleasure was as profound and as enduring. April 17, [1997,] marks the hundredth anniversary of Wilder's birth. The customary tributes are planned: a commemorative stamp is being issued, a Web site established, a Modern Library reader published. But the celebrations, I suspect, will be scattered and modest. Wilder's star, so bright on either side of World War II, has dimmed. For many readers nowadays, his name carries the faint whiff of the sachet,

From J.D. McClatchy, "Wilder and the Marvels of the Heart," *New York Times Book Review*, April 13, 1997. Copyright © 1997 by The New York Times Company. Reprinted by permission.

and his best work will seem sentimental and sententious to those who prefer their books braced with raw passions or caustic ironies.

THE WAY WE REMEMBER THE PAST

His best-known work remains *Our Town,* which was first performed in 1938 and has ever since been by far the most often produced American play. When Raymond Massey took it on tour to American G.I.'s in Europe in 1945, soon after the fighting had stopped, he reported that tears streamed down the faces of hardened soldiers. (They still stream down mine.) What undoubtedly touched those soldiers is the play's plangent nostalgia, the ache for home, for home's rootedness and security. But Wilder's portrait of the citizens of Grover's Corners, their lives and deaths, is not about the past so much as it is about the way we remember the past, what is illuminated and obscured by memory, gained and lost, the pathos of innocence, the sublimity of the ordinary, the acceptance of the dark ineluctable. And it is about what Wilder called "the eternal part" of us all. The religious reader will sense something more in that phrase. But Wilder himself would have called it the mind—an impulse, a characteristic, a power that sets us apart and onward.

To speak in such terms nowadays risks the sophisticate's smirk. Wilder stitched on homespun, and the result sometimes resembled the motto on a sampler. The instinct to generalize shouldn't be confused with softness. Wilder was no sentimentalist—a type, in his own definition, "whose desire that things be happy exceeds his desire and suppressed knowledge that things be truthful; he demands that he be lied to. He secretly knows that it is a lie; hence his emptiness, his elations and his heartlessness." Like [Oscar] Wilde or [Anton] Chekhov or [George Bernard] Shaw, he was essentially a moralist. Each of these playwrights could dramatize ideas and conduct, could make us think about our feelings. They sought, in their different ways, to clarify life by portraying its contradictions. Wilder took the given and raised it to the higher power of reflection. And he did it the hard way: by telling the truth.

A COMPLEX MAN

Wilder was a complex man. There are the plays and the novels, for which he was awarded three Pulitzer Prizes. But there is a great deal more. He had a profound respect for tradition and thought that literature "more resembled a torch race than a furious dispute among heirs." He was an erudite scholar of James Joyce and Lope de Vega, and lectured at both Harvard and the University of Chicago. He served in both world wars. He played the piano well enough to tackle the Beethoven sonatas, and wrote an opera libretto. He wrote screenplays for George Cukor, Alfred Hitchcock and Vittorio De Sica. He translated *A Doll's House* and *Waiting for Godot.* His published journals shimmer. He had a dizzyingly wide circle of friendships and counted among his acquaintances Gertrude Stein, Montgomery Clift, Coco Chanel, Sigmund Freud, Henry Luce, Alexander Woollcott, Laurence Olivier, Dorothy Parker, Jean-Paul Sartre, Tallulah Bankhead, Gene Tunney, Max Beerbohm, Felix Frankfurter, Ernest Hemingway and Sibyl Colefax.

He looked, Tyrone Guthrie said, like a piano tuner, owned only one suit at a time and spoke in a fidgety, accelerating, inexhaustible manner. He left all his domestic and business affairs for a devoted sister (his de facto "wife") to handle. He drank and smoked too much, was gregarious and self-effacing. He loathed self-pity. His compassion was clear-eyed and his generosities practical. He was endlessly obliging. Sylvia Beach said tartly that he reminded her of a man taking everyone in the world on a Sunday school picnic and trying to get them all on the bus at the same time. He especially liked helping old friends and talented beginners. He encouraged, for instance, a young actor named Orson Welles; and when the young Edward Albee was a fellow guest at Yaddo and busy writing poems, he remembers Wilder suggesting to him, "Why don't you try writing plays?" He was never without a new enthusiasm; even into his 70's, he was boning up on advances in microbiology, studying Greek vase painting or the theories of Claude Levi-Strauss.

Wilder seems to have been a repressed homosexual, baffled by his own desires and ashamed of his furtive attempts to act on them, and yet he made family life the arena of his imagination and wrote about it with a rare and compassionate understanding. Perhaps for this reason too, he cultivated the company of older, intelligent women as confidantes, hostesses, muses. He was a compulsive traveler and socializer, simultaneously to savor and to protect against a deep loneliness. His identical twin had died at birth, and there was a side to Wilder that was always restlessly searching to allay an unsatisfiable need. He had no "sturdy last resource against the occasional conviction 'I don't belong.'"

Myself, I prefer his novels to his plays. They haven't the accumulated glamour of those by [F. Scott] Fitzgerald and [Ernest] Hemingway and [William] Faulkner already in the pantheon. But the best of them remain remarkable accomplishments and deserve a wider audience. His first, *The Cabala* (1926), involves an Innocent Abroad, and is filled with worldly shrewdness and lapidary wit. It was an astonishing feat for a 29-year-old tyro, and won him instant acclaim. A year later he published *The Bridge of San Luis Rey.* With *The Woman of Andros* (1930) and *The Ides of March* (1948), Wilder upended the heavy social realism that dominated books of the day, and gave the exotic historical novel a genuine philosophical poise. But his two best novels have American settings. *Heaven's My Destination* (1935) is a picaresque comedy about the adventures of an itinerant textbook salesman, the earnest, self-righteous, Bible-thumping George Brush. *The Eighth Day* (1967) is a remarkable hybrid, part murder mystery, part family saga. Its hero, a mining engineer named John Ashley, is another of Wilder's unsettling anatomies of the fabled American innocence. Americans, he once said, are people who have outgrown their fathers. Like [Walt] Whitman's, Wilder's Americans are solitary, energetic, inventive, restless but disciplined, responsible but detached. They are one with the cold moonlight that falls equally on corpse and cradle, apple and ocean.

FINDING THE WONDROUS STRANGE IN THE ORDINARY

"I am not interested," he told an interviewer, "in the ephemeral—such subjects as the adulteries of dentists. I am interested in those things that repeat and repeat and repeat in the lives of the millions." He meant, of course, the mysteries and marvels of the heart. Wilder once described Tolstoy as "a great eye, above the roof, above the town, above the planet, from which nothing was hid." Wilder too looked on our life, steadily, never blinking at its pain and incongruities. But he was not a tortured artist or an embittered one. Instead, he was a master of high comedy. Into sorrows and convictions he mixed humor. In the ordinary he found what is wondrous strange. The tone of high comedy, he confided to his journal, is "lyrical, diaphanous and tender." If one added to those qualities a rueful joy and a deep humanity, then Wilder could be said to belong to a special group of artists—Jane Austen, Ivan Turgenev, Jean Renoir and Elizabeth Bishop are among them—whose work refreshes our intelligence. The older I get, and the more often I reread Wilder's novels, the brighter they seem, more subtle and courageous, filled with new surprises and earned wisdom.

Wilder's Tragic Themes

Robert W. Corrigan

Robert W. Corrigan has edited many anthologies on the
theater, including *The Art of the Theatre* and *The
Making of Theatre: From Drama to Performance;* his
own essays on theater are gathered in his anthology
The Theatre in Search of a Fix. Corrigan finds Wilder
the most difficult of modern American dramatists to
define. While all of Wilder's plays affirm life and celebrate love, Corrigan believes his view of life is essentially tragic. Since he presents tragedy in an everyday context, which is often not dramatic, many critics have
failed to comprehend his true beliefs. Yet, Corrigan
acknowledges, Wilder manages to avoid despair with
an "animal faith" that is stronger than logical argument.

Of all modern American dramatists, none is more difficult to
pin down than Thornton Wilder. He is thought of, together
with [Eugene] O'Neill, [Arthur] Miller, and [Tennessee]
Williams, as one of our "Big Four," and yet his reputation is
based on only three full-length plays and was made on one.
And whereas reams of criticism have been written on the
other three playwrights, only an occasional article on Wilder
is published. This is all the more surprising since no one
seems to agree about his work. For some he is the great
American satirist; for others he is a soft-hearted sentimentalist; and for still others he is our only "religious" dramatist.
Furthermore, no American playwright is more respected by
contemporary European dramatists than is Wilder; Brecht,
Ionesco, Duerrenmatt, and Frisch have all acknowledged
their debt to this "great and fanatical experimenter."
Therefore, it is about time that we reevaluate his work.

DEISTIC PLATONISM, NOT CHRISTIANITY

From his earliest volumes of one-acts, *The Angel that
Troubled the Waters* and *The Long Christmas Dinner*, to his

From "Thornton Wilder and the Tragic Sense of Life," by Robert W. Corrigan,
Educational Theatre Journal, vol. 13, no. 3 (1961). Copyright © 1961 by the American
Theatre Association, Inc. Reprinted by permission of the Johns Hopkins University Press.

last full-length play, *The Matchmaker,* Wilder has dealt bold-
ly and affirmatively with the themes of Life, Love, and Earth.
Each of his plays is a hymn in dramatic form affirming life.
But the important question is: What is the nature of this
affirmation? It is not, as some would have it, Christian. To
begin with, Wilder has no belief—at least as expressed in his
plays—in a religion that is revealed or historical. These are
basic premises of Christianity. To be sure Wilder is deistic,
but as almost all of his critics have pointed out, he is essentially a religious Platonist; and this position must ultimately
reject the historic dimension as meaningful. Francis
Fergusson ties these two ideas together when he writes:

> The plays are perfectly in accord with the Platonic kind of
> philosophy which they are designed to teach. The great Ideas
> are timeless, above the history of the race and the history of
> actual individuals. Any bit of individual or racial history will
> do, therefore, to "illustrate" them; but history and individual
> lives lack all real being; they are only shadows on the cave
> wall.

Mary McCarthy approaches this another way when she
writes of *The Skin of Our Teeth:*

> In other words, if George misses the five-fifteen, Chaos is
> come again. This is the moral of the piece. Man, says Mr.
> Wilder, from time to time gets puffed up with pride and pros-
> perity, he grows envious, covetous, lecherous, forgets his
> conjugal duties, goes whoring after women; portents of dis-
> aster appear, but he is too blind to see them; in the end, with
> the help of the little woman, who has never taken any stock
> in either pleasure or wisdom, he escapes by the skin of his
> teeth. *Sicut erat in principio* [as it was in the beginning]. . . .
>
> It is a curious view of life. It displays elements of Christian
> morality. Christ, however, was never so simple, but on the
> contrary allowed always for paradox (the woman taken in
> adultery, the story of Martha and Mary, "Consider the lilies of
> the field"). . . . No, it is not the Christian view, but a kind of
> bowdlerized version of it, such as might have been imparted
> to a class of taxpayer's children by a New England Sunday
> School teacher forty years ago.

Now, I happen to believe that both Fergusson and Miss
McCarthy (even in their admiration for Wilder) overstate
their arguments, because Wilder, except in his preface to
The Angel that Troubled the Waters, has never thought of
himself as a Christian or a religious playwright. He best
states his position when he writes: "*Our Town* is not offered
as a picture of life in a New Hampshire village; or specula-

tion about the conditions of life after death. . . . It is an attempt to find a value above all price for the smallest events of daily life." Wilder is talking about *Our Town*, but what he says applies to all of his work. In short, Wilder is a humanist, an affirming humanist, a "yeasayer to life" as Barnard Hewitt calls him.

LOVE AND DEATH

When we examine the nature of Wilder's humanistic affirmations, what do we discover? His plays celebrate human love, the worth and dignity of man, the values of the ordinary, and the eternity of human values. From the little boy in Wilder's first play who says: "I am not afraid of life. I will astonish it!" to Dolly Levi and her cohorts in adventure in *The Matchmaker*, Wilder has always been on the side of life and life is seen to be most directly affirmed through love. Love, then, is his most persistent theme and it has been for him an inexhaustible subject. Of its worth he is convinced, but it is interesting to note that Wilder has never been able to make any commitments as to the reasons for its worth. Wilder can deal with life and love directly and concretely; but when he moves to the edges of life, the focus becomes less sharp. Certainly, Wilder deals with death—he is not afraid of it, but death in his plays is terminal. When Mrs. Soames says in Act Three of *Our Town:* "My, wasn't life awful—and wonderful," Wilder is reminding us that beauty is recognizable because of change and life is meaningful because of death. But as both John Mason Brown and Winfield Townley Scott have pointed out, Wilder never deals adequately with Death's own meaning. And as for what's beyond death? The Stage Manager in *Our Town* tells us:

> You know as well as I do that the dead don't stay interested in us living people for very long. Gradually, gradually, they let go of the earth. . . . They get weaned away from the earth— that's the way I put it—weaned away. Yes, they stay here while the earth-part of 'em burns away, burns out, and all that time they slowly get indifferent to what's going on in Grover's Corners. They're waitin'! They're waitin' for something that they feel is comin'. Something important and great. Aren't they waitin' for the eternal part in them to come out clear?

But what is this eternal part, this Platonic essence, which in our imperfect awareness of living is only a shadow on the wall of the cave? What is death's meaning? The Stage Manager has just told us:

> Everybody knows that *something* is eternal. And it ain't
> names, and it ain't earth, and it ain't even the stars . . . every-
> body knows in their bones that *something* is eternal, and that
> something has to do with human beings. All the greatest peo-
> ple ever lived have been telling us that for five thousand years
> and yet you'd be surprised how people are always losing hold
> of it. There's something way down deep that's eternal about
> every human being.

So, we are right back where we started: Life is reality and
eternity is the perfected essence of that reality to which we
are too often blind and of which we can't stand too much.

A TRAGIC VIEW OF LIFE

It is this tendency, a tendency consistent with his Platonism,
to reduce the dimension of eternity so that it can be encom-
passed by life itself, that has led me to believe, although he
has written no tragedies, that Wilder has essentially a tragic
rather than a Christian or even religious view of life. To be
sure, Wilder has not created any Ahabs or Lears, but this is
not because he lacks a tragic vision. He happens to believe,
as did Maeterlinck, that there are times in each of our lives
when we are conscious of moving into the boundary situations of the tragic realm, and that furthermore, life's tragedies
can best be seen in the drama of the everyday, in life's smallest events. For this reason he does not dramatize great conflicts in order to capture the quintessence of tragedy. I think
it is important to see the validity of this, although we must
point out that while this approach is tragic it is not always
dramatic. And this, I think, accounts for the fact that Wilder's
plays are usually referred to as "hymns," "odes," "songs," and
so on, and most critics feel that there isn't much conflict in
their plots. It might be helpful to take a specific example to
illustrate Wilder's position on this matter.

Over and over again in Wilder's work, the belief is stated
directly and indirectly that "life is what you make of it." The
fullest discussion of the idea is in his novel *The Ides of
March,* where Caesar says: "Life has no meaning save that
which we confer upon it." Later he says:

> Am I sure that there is no mind behind our existence and no
> mystery anywhere in the universe? I think I am. . . . How ter-
> rifying and glorious the role of man if, indeed, without guid-
> ance and without consolation he must create from his own
> vitals the meaning for his existence and the rules whereby he
> lives.

Many of us believe this idea when stated in its simpler form: "Life is what we make of it." But we are unaware that this is really an existential position and that Wilder is very close to Sartre's "Man is condemned to be free."

AVERTING DESPAIR THROUGH ANIMAL FAITH

In fact, upon reflection, we discover that in starting from "Life is what we make of it," Wilder is really in the mainstream of the modern drama beginning with Ibsen and Strindberg. And this is a dangerous position and usually in the drama has led to despair. The image of man in this drama is an image of collapse. Certainly, Kierkegaard saw this in [this] passage from *Fear and Trembling:*

> If there were no eternal consciousness in a man, if at the foundation of all there lay only a wildly seething power which writhing with obscure passions produced everything that is great and everything that is insignificant, if a bottomless void never satiated lay hidden beneath all—what then would life be but despair.

Most modern dramatists have answered with "that's all!" But Wilder hasn't, even though he holds a position that should lead this way. I think he averts despair—and also tragedy, even though his view of life is essentially tragic—with a kind of Santayana-like belief in life. In fact, Wilder's Platonism can make sense only if it is seen as coming through Santayana.[1] Wilder is, as probably most of us are, saved from despair and its paralyzing effects by what Santayana has called "animal faith." Many will admit that by the rules of logic life is little more than an irrational nightmare in which the only reality is that grotesque illusion which we happen to believe in at a given moment; but somehow our animal faith, which bids us believe in the external world, is much stronger than all the logical arguments which tend to make life seem absurd. As Joseph Wood Krutch put it: "Everybody acts as though he believed that the external world exists; nearly everybody acts as though he believed that his version of it is a dependable one; and the majority act as though they could also make valid value judgments about it." It is this belief, this animal faith, that permits Wilder to say "Life is what you make of it," and still come up in affirmation on this side of despair. All his plays might be described by that

1. George Santayana (1863–1952), poet and philosopher born in Madrid, Spain; wrote several volumes of verse, and philosophical works including *Scepticism and Animal Faith* (1923).

verse of Theodore Spencer's (and I think Wilder and Spencer have great affinities):

Oh how to praise that No,
When all longing would press
After the lost Yes!
Oh how redress
That disaster of No?

But although Wilder can assert meaning to life, the meaning is almost in the assertion itself and this is not a very comfortable position to be in. One gets the feeling that Wilder has to keep saying it to make sure that it is true. The danger of this position is that it lacks the necessary polarity and tension for full meaning. This in itself keeps Wilder from being a religious dramatist. In all great religious drama—the works of Sophocles, Calderón, *Everyman,* and in more recent times the later plays of Hofmannsthal, Eliot, and even Fry—there is the backdrop of religious belief which gives meaning to and informs the hero's "life is what you make of it." There is the greater stage. The medieval theatre and the Spanish theatre of Calderón exhibit this, and this is what Hofmannsthal tried to achieve at the Salzburg festivals with his productions of *Everyman, The Great World Theatre,* and *The Tower.* In all of these plays the actors—man—are faced with a moral choice under the very eyes of God and his angels upstage. The scaffold of these multiple stage structures not only serves as a magic mirror for the visible world and its invisible order, but the invisible order is made visible. For in these plays the idea of man as a player on the world's stage becomes the very principle of the *mise-en-scène* [stage setting]. For God, the master, speaking from the top of the scaffold, actually orders the world to produce a play under his eyes, featuring man who is to act out his part on earth.

REDUCING THE SENSE OF DRAMATIC PLACE AND TIME

More important than the absence of a religious dimension to Wilder's work, however, are the many experiments he has made in theatrical technique to compensate for this lack of an ultimate perspective. It is a commonplace in talking about modern literature to comment on the loss of a community of values and the disappearance of public truths in our time. It is equally well known that writers tend to compensate for the lack of a community of belief with new tech-

FOUR FUNDAMENTAL CONDITIONS OF DRAMA

In "Some Thoughts on Playwrighting," Wilder explained some of his views on the theater. His elaborations on these points bring in references to painters, dancers, and novelists as well as dramatists.

Four fundamental conditions of the drama separate it from the other arts. Each of these conditions has its advantages and disadvantages, each requires a particular aptitude from the dramatist, and from each there are a number of instructive consequences to be derived. These conditions are:

1. The theater is an art which reposes upon the work of many collaborators;
2. It is addressed to the group-mind;
3. It is based upon a pretense and its very nature calls out a multiplication of pretenses;
4. Its action takes place in a perpetual present time.

Thornton Wilder, "Some Thoughts on Playwrighting," in Augusto Centeno, ed., *The Intent of the Artist.* New York: Russell & Russell, 1970.

niques of expression. The problem for the dramatist is how to make a highly individual standard of values appear to the audience to be a natural objective standard. Most of the modern dramatists have attempted to meet this problem by focusing on the psychology of their characters. In so doing they leave begged the question of value by confining the world of the play to the limits of an individual character's mind and then assessing value solely in terms of the consciousness of that mind. Thus, an incident in *Hedda Gabler* may not be important by any communicable standard of human significance, but if the universe is confined to her mind and Ibsen makes us look deeply enough into it, we can at least see it as important in that tiny context. In this way psychology makes possible such a drastic limitation of context that a private world can be the subject of a tragedy. Furthermore, by new techniques of presentation that private world and its values can be made, at least for the duration of the performance, convincing.

Wilder has not been interested in psychology and has never used psychological techniques to solve the "modernists'" problems in the theatre. This accounts, I think, for his great influence on the Continental avant-garde dramatists who are rebelling against our psychologically oriented theatre. Wilder sought to achieve the sense of an ultimate perspective by immaterializing the sense of dramatic place on stage. The bare stage of *Our Town* with its chairs, tables, and ladders, together with the Stage Manager's bald exposition, are all that he uses to create the town. The same is true of *The Skin of Our Teeth;* you never really know where the Antrobuses live, nor when. This is his second dominant technique; by destroying the illusion of time, Wilder achieves the effect of any time, all time, each time. But this is risky business, for without the backdrop of an ultimate perspective to inform a play's action, it can very easily become sentimental or satirical, or even pretentious. Wilder at his best keeps this from happening, but his only weapons are wit and irony. And a production which does not succeed in capturing these qualities (as, alas, most college and school productions do not) is bound to turn out bathetic and sentimental; when technique is used as a compensation for the ultimate perspective, the resultant work of art always lies precariously under a Damoclean sword.

A TRAGIC SENSE OF DESTINY

It is important that we see the dangers in Wilder's methods, but that a tragic sense of life informs his plays is best illustrated by his sense of destiny. In Wilder's novel *The Woman of Andros,* Chrysis tells her guests a fable of the dead hero who receives Zeus's permission to return to earth to relive the least eventful day of his life, on the condition that he see it both as onlooker and participant.

> Suddenly the hero saw that the living too are dead and that we can only be said to be alive in those moments when our hearts are conscious of our treasure; for our hearts are not strong enough to love every moment.

He quickly asks to be released from this experience, and it is the opinion of Chrysis that

> All human beings—save a few mysterious exceptions who seemed to be in possession of some secret from the gods— merely endured the slow misery of existence, hiding as best they could their consternation that life had no wonderful surprises after all and that its most difficult burden was the incommunicability of love.

Eight years later Wilder incorporated this into the last scene of *Our Town.* When Emily comes back on her twelfth birthday, she discovers that "we don't have time to look at one another. I didn't realize. So all that was going on and we

never noticed. . . . Oh, earth you're too wonderful for anybody to realize you. Do any human beings ever realize life
while they live it?—every, every minute?" The answer, of
course, is no, and Emily must conclude with "That's all
human beings are! Just blind people."

What Wilder is saying here is that human beings cannot
stand to have a sense of destiny—the awareness that there is
a continuity in all our acts, the awareness that every present
moment comes from a past and is directed to a future. Only
at moments, usually of emotional crisis, do we have this
sense of destiny, this sense of awareness of the future. It is
this sense of destiny that is the great human reality and the
tragedy of life lies in our fragmentary and imperfect awareness of it. Wilder is aware, like Eliot, that "human kind cannot bear very much reality," but his plays fall short of
tragedy because he takes the Platonic escape, he moves into
a world that denies the reality and the nemesis of destiny.
Nor does he have the solution of an Eliot. For in denying,
finally, the reality of destiny he shuts out the possibility of
ever providing the means to perfect our fragmentary and
imperfect vision. He fails, to use Karl Jaspers' phrase, to go
"Beyond Tragedy." That Wilder lacks this dimension is not to
discredit him, however, for no other American dramatist
more fully affirms that miracle of life which so much modern drama would deny.

Morality in Wilder's Work

Malcolm Cowley

Malcolm Cowley, author of Exile's Return: A Literary
Odyssey of the 1920s, *has written widely about his
contemporaries, the members of the so-called Lost
Generation—American writers who first published
in the decade or so after World War I. In this essay,
Cowley finds fundamental differences between
Thornton Wilder and the other writers of his time.
While most of the members of the Lost Generation
wrote about social groups, Cowley notes, Wilder was
concerned with individuals. Yet at the same time
Wilder found universal patterns in human experience that could be illustrated in the lives of people of
any place or time.*

There is a . . . fundamental difference between [Thornton
Wilder's] work and that of his contemporaries. The others
write novels about a social group—sometimes a small group,
as in [F. Scott Fitzgerald's] *Tender Is the Night,* sometimes a
very large one, as in [John Dos Passos's] *U.S.A.*—or they write
about an individual in revolt against the group, as in [Ernest
Hemingway's] *A Farewell to Arms.* The central relation with
which they deal is between the many and the one. Very often—
to borrow a pair of terms from David Riesman—their theme is
the defeat of an inner-directed hero by an other-directed society. They feel that the society and its standards must be carefully portrayed, and these writers are all, to some extent, novelists of manners.—Wilder is a novelist of morals.

Manners and morals are terms that overlap, sometimes
confusingly, but here I am using the two words in senses that
are easier to distinguish. Manners would be the standards of
conduct that prevail in a group, large or small, and hence they
would change from group to group and year to year. Morals

would be defined as the standards that determine the relations of individuals with other individuals, one with one—a child with each of its parents, a husband with his wife, a rich man with a poor man (not *the* rich with *the* poor)—and also the relations of any man with himself, his destiny, and his God. They are answers found by individuals to the old problems of faith, hope, charity or love, art, duty, submission to one's fate . . . and hence they are relatively universal; they can be illustrated from the lives of any individuals, in any place, at any time since the beginning of time.

THE GREAT UNSOCIAL AND ANTIHISTORICAL NOVELIST

The characters in Wilder's novels and plays are looking for such answers; his work is not often concerned with the behavior of groups. An outstanding exception might be *Our Town* (1938), in which the Stage Manager speaks with the voice of the community. But the community hasn't much to say about itself and will not admit to having local color; it might be any town, a fact that explains the success of the play in towns all over the country, and other countries. The events portrayed are coming of age, falling in love, getting married, and dying; in other words they are not truly events—except for the characters, who are not truly characters—but rather they serve as examples of a universal pattern in human lives; and they are not greatly affected, in the play, by the special manners of this one community. *The Cabala* (1926) also starts by dealing with a group, but very soon the young American narrator shifts his attention to its separate members, explaining that he is "the biographer of the individuals and not the historian of the group." The statement applies to the author himself, and in a simpler form: Wilder is not a historian. In Rome he had studied archaeology and had learned to look backward and forward through a long vista of years; that sort of vision is a special quality of all his work. But what he sees at the end of a vista is what the archaeologist often sees, that is, fragments of a finished pattern of life in many ways similar to our own. It is not what the historian tries to see: a living community in a process of continual and irreversible change.

The other novelists of his generation are all in some way historians. Their basic perception was of the changes in their own time, from peace to war, from stability to instability, from a fixed code of behavior to the feeling that "It's all right if you can get away with it." For them the Great War was a true event, in the sense that afterward nothing was the same. All of them were "haunted fatally by the sense of time," as [Thomas] Wolfe says of his autobiographical hero. His second novel was *Of Time and the River.* Hemingway's first book was *In Our Time* and he let it be understood, ". . . as in no other time." [William] Faulkner saw his time in the South as one of violent decay. When Dos Passos tried to put thirty years of American life into one big novel, he invented a device called the Newsreel, intended to convey the local color of each particular year. Fitzgerald put the same sort of material into the body of his stories; he wrote as if with an eye on the calendar. *The Great Gatsby* belongs definitely to the year 1923, when the Fitzgeralds were living in Great Neck, Long Island, and *Tender Is the Night* could have ended only in 1930; no other year on the Riviera had quite the same atmosphere of things going to pieces. Both books are historical novels about his own time, so accurately observed, so honestly felt, that the books are permanent.—Wilder would never attempt to draw such a picture of his time. He is the great unsocial and antihistorical novelist, the master of the anachronism.

THE VAST LANDSCAPE OF TIME

Like Dos Passos he gives us a newsreel, or rather two of them, to introduce the first two acts of *The Skin of Our Teeth* (1942). The contrast here is complete. Where Dos Passos recalls such episodes as the capture of the bobbed-hair bandit, the Florida real-estate boom, and the suppression of a revolt in Canton (to the refrain of "I'm Dancing with Tears in My Eyes"), Wilder presents another order of phenomena. Before the first act, when the lights go out, the name of the theater flashes on the screen and we hear the Announcer's voice:

> The management takes pleasure in bringing to you—the news of the world! (*Slide 2. The sun appearing above the horizon.*) Freeport, Long Island. The sun rose this morning at 6:32 a.m. This gratifying event was first reported by (*Slide 3*) Mrs. Dorothy Stetson of Freeport, Long Island, who promptly telephoned the Mayor. The Society for Affirming (*Slide 4*) the End of the World at once went into a special session and postponed the arrival of that event for *twenty-four hours* (*Slide 5*). All honor to Mrs. Stetson for her public spirit.
>
> New York City. (*Slide 6, of the front doors of the theater.*) The Plymouth Theater. During the daily cleaning of this theater a number of lost objects were collected, as usual (*Slide 7*), by Mesdames Simpson, Pateslewski, and Moriarity. Among these

objects found today was (*Slide 8*) a wedding ring, inscribed: To Eve from Adam. Genesis 2:18. The ring will be restored to the owner or owners, if their credentials are satisfactory.

Wilder's news of the world is first what happens every day, and then what happened at the beginning. In all his work—except for that hint of the Creation—I can think of only one event that marks a change in human affairs: it is the birth of Christ, as announced on the first and the last page of *The Woman of Andros* (1930). Perhaps another event is foreshadowed in a much later novel, *The Eighth Day* (1967): it is the birth of new messiahs, something that might resemble a Second Coming. That other Christian event, the Fall, is nowhere mentioned and seems to play no part in Wilder's theology. Everything else in his plays and novels— even the collapse of a famous bridge—is merely an example or illustration of man's universal destiny. Nothing is unique, the author seems to be saying; the Ice Age will return, as will the Deluge, as will Armageddon. After each disaster man will start over again—helped by his books, if he has saved them—and will struggle upward until halted by a new disaster. "Rome existed before Rome," the shade of Virgil says at the end of *The Cabala*, "and when Rome will be a waste there will be Romes after her." "There are no Golden Ages and no Dark Ages," we read in *The Eighth Day*. "There is the oceanlike monotony of the generations of men under the alternations of fair and foul weather." The same book says, "It is only in appearance that time is a river. It is rather a vast landscape and it is the eye of the beholder that moves."

UNIVERSALLY SHARED EXPERIENCE AND ETERNAL RETURN

At this point I think we might glimpse a design that unites what Wilder has written from beginning to end. He has published not quite a dozen books, each strikingly different from all the others in place, in time, in social setting, and even more in method, yet all the books illustrate the same feeling of universally shared experience and eternal return. *Everything that happened might happen anywhere and will happen again.* That principle explains why he is able to adopt different perspectives in different books, as though he were looking sometimes through one end of a telescope, sometimes through the other. In *The Ides of March* (1948) a distant object is magnified and Rome in 45 B.C. is described as if it were New York two thousand years later. In *Our Town* he reverses the telescope and shows us Grover's Corners as if it had been preserved for two thousand years under a lava flow and then unearthed like Herculaneum. He has many other fashions of distorting time. *The Long Christmas Dinner* (1931) is a one-act play in which the dinner lasts for ninety years, with members of the family appearing from a bright door and going out through a dark door, to indicate birth and death. *The Skin of Our Teeth* epitomizes the story of mankind in three acts and four characters: Adam, Eve, Lilith, and Cain. They are living in Excelsior, New Jersey, when the glacial cap comes grinding down on them. In Atlantic City, just before the Deluge, they launch an ark full of animals two by two from the Million Dollar Pier.

Because Wilder denies the importance of time, his successive books have proved to be either timely or untimely in a spectacular fashion—and in both cases by accident. *The Bridge of San Luis Rey* (1927) exactly fitted the mood of the moment, and nobody knows exactly why. *The Woman of Andros* was published thirty years too late or too soon. *The Skin of Our Teeth* had a more complicated history. Produced on Broadway in 1942, it was a success largely because of Tallulah Bankhead's so-jolly part of Lilith, or Lily Sabina. Hardly anyone said that the play expressed the mood of the moment, or of any other moment. But when it was staged in Central Europe after World War II, it was not only a success but a historic one, for any cast of actors that played in it. The Germans and the Austrians seem to have felt that it was a topical drama written especially for them, to soften their defeat and give them strength to live.

The Skin of Our Teeth is derived in part from [James Joyce's] *Finnegans Wake*, as *The Woman of Andros* is based in part on Terence's[1] *Andria*, and as the plot of *The Bridge* was suggested by one of Mérimée's[2] shorter plays. We read in a note on *The Matchmaker* (1954), "This play is based upon a comedy by Johann Nestroy, *Einen Jux Will Er Sich Machen* (Vienna, 1842), which was in turn based upon an English original, *A Day Well Spent*, by John Oxenford." There are many other acknowledged derivations in Wilder's work, from authors of many times and countries, and together they reveal another aspect of his disregard for history. He feels that a true author is independent of time and

1. Roman playwright of the second century B.C. 2. French writer Prosper Mérimée, 1803–1870.

country, and he also feels, apparently, that there is no history of literature, but only a pattern consisting of books that continue to live because they contain permanent truths. Any new author is at liberty to restate those truths and to borrow plots or methods from older authors, so long as he transforms the borrowed material into something of his own. Not only was every great book written this morning, but it can be read tonight as on the first day. That principle, in two of Wilder's plays, becomes a metaphor that is a masterpiece of foreshortening. In a one-acter called *Pullman Car Hiawatha* and again in the third act of *The Skin of Our Teeth*, the great philosophers are presented as hours of the night. One of the characters explains: "Just like the hours and stars go by over our heads at night, in the same way the ideas and thoughts of the great men are in the air around us all the time and they're working on us, even when we don't know it." Spinoza is nine o'clock, Plato is ten, Aristotle is eleven, and Moses is midnight. Three thousand years of thought are reduced to four hours, which pass in less than two minutes on the stage.

This foreshortening of time becomes an opportunity for the novelist as well as for the playwright. When history is regarded as a recurrent pattern rather than as a process, it becomes possible to move a character from almost any point in time or space to almost any other. In *The Bridge* Mme. de Sévigné[3] reappears in Peru as the Marquesa de Montemayor. [John] Keats is presented in *The Cabala*, with his genius, his illness, his family problems; and he dies again in 1920 among a group of strange characters who might be resurrected from the *Memoirs* of the Duc de Saint-Simon,[4] or who also might be classical gods and goddesses in modern dress. Persons can be moved backward in time as well as forward. Edward Sheldon,[5] the crippled and blinded dramatist who lived for thirty years in retirement, dispensing wisdom to his friends, appears in *The Ides of March* as Lucius Manilius Turrinus, and one suspects that Cicero, in the same novel, is a preincarnation of Alexander Woollcott.[6] As for the hero of the novel, he is not a historical character but a model or paradigm of the man of decision, as such a man might exist in any age. Wilder has called him Julius Caesar, much as Paul

3. French writer, especially of letters, 1626–1696. 4. French philosopher and social scientist, founder of French socialism, 1760–1825. 5. American playwright, 1886–1946. 6. American journalist, writer, drama critic, 1887–1943.

Valéry called his man of intellect Leonardo da Vinci, and much as [Ralph Waldo] Emerson gave the title of "Plato" to his essay on man as philosopher.

EMERSONIAN TRANSCENDENTALISM

So Emerson's name comes up again, as it did in the case of e.e. cummings (though it wouldn't make sense to mention the name in connection with any other writer of the Lost Generation). Emerson was of course the prophet who gave no importance to groups or institutions and refused to think of history as a process. When he discussed Montaigne[7] or Shakespeare, it was not against the background of their times, but rather as "representative men" whom he might meet at any dinner of the Saturday Club. Wilder, in the brilliant series of lectures that he gave at Harvard in 1950–51, started with Emerson, [Henry David] Thoreau, and other classical American writers, notably [Herman] Melville and [Walt] Whitman. What he tried to deduce from their works was the character of the representative American, but what he actually presented was, I suspect, partly a reflection of his own character. Here are some of his statements:

> From the point of view of the European an American is nomad in relation to place, disattached in relation to time, lonely in relation to society, and insubmissive to circumstances, destiny, or God.

> Americans could count and enjoyed counting. They lived under a sense of boundlessness. . . . To this day, in American thinking, a crowd of ten thousand is not a homogeneous mass of that number, but is one and one and one . . . up to ten thousand.

> Since the American can find no confirmation of identity from the environment in which he lives, since he lives exposed to the awareness of vast distances and innumerable existences, since he derives from a belief in the future the courage that animates him, is he not bent on isolating and "fixing" a value on every existing thing in its relation to a totality, to the All, to the Everywhere, to the Always?

Those are perceptive statements, but I should question whether they apply to most Americans today, or to many American writers since the First World War. Their primary application is to all the big and little Emersonians, beginning with Thoreau (who is Wilder's favorite) and Whitman. In our own day they apply to Wilder himself more than to

7. French essayist, 1533–1592.

any other writer—more than to Cummings, even, whose later work revives the Emersonian tradition, but chiefly on its romantic, mystical, anarchistic side. Wilder is neoclassical, as I said. He goes back to Pope[8] and Addison[9] in his attitude toward the art of letters, but in other habits of thought he clearly goes back to the Transcendentalists. His work has more than a little of the moral distinction they tried to achieve, and like their work it deals with the relation of one to one, or of anyone to the All, the Everywhere, and the Always. Like theirs it looks toward the future with confidence, though not with the bland confidence that some of the Emersonians displayed. "Every human being who has existed can be felt by us as existing now," Wilder says in another of his Norton lectures, as if to explain his foreshortening of history. "All time is present for a single time. . . . Many problems which now seem insoluble will be solved when the world realizes that we are all bound together as the population of the only inhabited star."

---

8. Alexander Pope, 1688–1744, English poet. 9. Joseph Addison, 1672–1719, English essayist and poet.

Plays That Portray the Truth of Human Existence

Thornton Wilder

Asked to write a preface for a collection of three of his plays—*Our Town, The Skin of Our Teeth,* and *The Matchmaker*—Wilder took the opportunity to discuss his dissatisfactions with contemporary theater. The aristocracy had limited the theater, he explains, but it was the rise of the middle class that turned a vibrant art into an inconsequential diversion. The new middle class's desire for a "soothing" experience led to audience detachment. Wilder shows how his plays are an attempt to return the passion to the theater.

Toward the end of the 'twenties I began to lose pleasure in going to the theatre. I ceased to believe in the stories I saw presented there. When I did go it was to admire some secondary aspect of the play, the work of a great actor or director or designer. Yet at the same time the conviction was growing in me that the theatre was the greatest of all the arts. I felt that something had gone wrong with it in my time and that it was fulfilling only a small part of its potentialities. I was filled with admiration for presentations of classical works by Max Reinhardt and Louis Jouvet and the Old Vic, as I was by the best plays of my time, like *Desire Under the Elms* and *The Front Page;* but it was with a grudging admiration, for at heart *I didn't believe a word of them.* I was like a schoolmaster grading a paper; to each of these offerings I gave an A+, but the condition of mind of one grading a paper is not that of one being overwhelmed by an artistic creation. The response we make when we "believe" a work of the imagination is that of saying: "This is the way things are. I have always known it without being fully aware that I knew it.

Now in the presence of this play or novel or poem (or picture or piece of music) I know that I know it." It is this form of knowledge which Plato called "recollection." We have all murdered, in thought; and been murdered. We have all seen the ridiculous in estimable persons and in ourselves. We have all known terror as well as enchantment. Imaginative literature has nothing to say to those who do not recognize— who cannot be *reminded*—of such conditions. Of all the arts the theatre is best endowed to awaken this recollection within us—to believe is to say "yes"; but in theatres of my time I did not feel myself prompted to any such grateful and self-forgetting acquiescence.

This dissatisfaction worried me. I was not ready to condemn myself as blasé and over-fastidious, for I knew that I was still capable of belief. I believed every word of *Ulysses* and of Proust and of *The Magic Mountain*, as I did of hundreds of plays when I read them. It was on the stage that imaginative narration became false. Finally, my dissatisfaction passed into resentment. I began to feel that the theatre was not only inadequate, it was evasive; it did not wish to draw upon its deeper potentialities. I found the word for it: it aimed to be *soothing*. The tragic had no heat; the comic had no bite; the social criticism failed to indict us with responsibility.

I began to search for the point where the theatre had run off the track, where it had chosen—and been permitted—to become a minor art and an inconsequential diversion.

The trouble began in the nineteenth century and was connected with the rise of the middle classes—they wanted their theatre soothing. There's nothing wrong with the middle classes in themselves. We know that now. The United States and Scandinavia and Germany are middle-class countries, so completely so that they have lost the very memory of their once despised and ludicrous inferiority (they had been inferior not only to the aristocracy but, in human dignity, to the peasantry). When a middle class is new, however, there is much that is wrong with it. When it is emerging under the shadow of an aristocracy, from the myth and prestige of those well-born Higher-ups, it is alternately insecure and aggressively complacent. It must find its justification and reassurance in making money and displaying it. To this day, members of the middle classes in England, France, and Italy feel themselves to be a little ridiculous and humiliated.

The prestige of aristocracies is based upon a dreary

untruth: that moral superiority and the qualifications for leadership are transmittable through the chromosomes, and the secondary lie, that the environment afforded by privilege and leisure tends to nurture the flowers of the spirit. An aristocracy, defending and fostering its lie, extracts from the arts only such elements as can further its interests, the aroma and not the sap, the grace and not the trenchancy.

Equally harmful to culture is the newly arrived middle class. In the English-speaking world the middle classes came into power early in the nineteenth century and gained control over the theatre. They were pious, law-abiding, and industrious. They were assured of eternal life in the next world and, in this, they were squarely seated on Property and the privileges that accompany it. They were attended by devoted servants who knew their place. They were benevolent within certain limits, but chose to ignore wide tracts of injustice and stupidity in the world about them; and they shrank from contemplating those elements within themselves that were ridiculous, shallow, and harmful. They distrusted the passions and tried to deny them. Their questions about the nature of life seemed to be sufficiently answered by the demonstration of financial status and by conformity to some clearly established rule of decorum. These were precarious positions; abysses yawned on either side. The air was loud with questions that must not be asked.

These middle-class audiences fashioned a theatre which could not disturb them. They thronged to melodrama (which deals with tragic possibilities in such a way that you know from the beginning that all will end happily) and to sentimental drama (which accords a total license to the supposition that the wish is father to the thought) and to comedies in which the characters were so represented that they always resembled someone else and not oneself. Between the plays that Sheridan wrote in his twenties and the first works of Wilde and Shaw there was no play of even moderate interest written in the English language. (Unless you happen to admire and except Shelley's *The Cenci.*) These audiences, however, also thronged to Shakespeare. How did they shield themselves against his probing? How did they smother the theatre—and with such effect that it smothers us still? The box-set was already there, the curtain, the proscenium, but not taken "seriously"—it was a convenience in view of the weather in northern countries. They took it seriously and emphasized and enhanced everything that thus removed, cut off, and boxed the action; they increasingly shut the play up into a museum showcase.

Let us examine why the box-set stage stifles the life in drama and why and how it militates against belief.

JUGGLING WITH TIME

Every action which has ever taken place—every thought, every emotion—has taken place only once, at one moment in time and place. "I love you," "I rejoice," "I suffer," have been said and felt many billions of times, and never twice the same. Every person who has ever lived has lived an unbroken succession of unique occasions. Yet the more one is aware of this individuality in experience (innumerable! innumerable!) the more one becomes attentive to what these disparate moments have in common, to repetitive patterns. As an artist (or listener or beholder) which "truth" do you prefer—that of the isolated occasion, or that which includes and resumes the innumerable? Which truth is more worth telling? Every age differs in this. Is the Venus de Milo "one woman"? Is the play *Macbeth* the story of "one destiny"? The theatre is admirably fitted to tell both truths. It has one foot planted firmly in the particular, since each actor before us (even when he wears a mask!) is indubitably a living breathing "one"; yet it tends and strains to exhibit a general truth since its relation to a specific "realistic" truth is confused and undermined by the fact that it is an accumulation of untruths, pretenses, and fiction.

All the arts depend on preposterous fictions, but the theatre is the most preposterous of all. Imagine asking us to believe that we are in Venice in the sixteenth century, and that Mr. Billington is a Moor, and that he is about to stifle the much-admired Miss Huckaby with a pillow; and imagine trying to make us believe that people ever talked in blank verse—more than that: that people were ever so marvelously articulate. The theatre is a lily that inexplicably arises from a jungle of weedy falsities. Yet it is precisely from the tension produced by all this absurdity, "contrary to fact," that it is able to create such poetry, power, enchantment, and truth.

The novel is pre-eminently the vehicle of the unique occasion, the theatre of the generalized one. It is through the theatre's power to raise the exhibited individual action into the realm of idea and type and universal that it is able to evoke our belief. But power is precisely what those nineteenth-century audiences did not—dared not—confront. They tamed it and drew its teeth; squeezed it into that removed showcase. They loaded the stage with specific objects, because every concrete object on the stage fixes and narrows the action to one moment in time and place. (Have you ever noticed that in the plays of Shakespeare no one—except occasionally a ruler—ever sits down? There were not even chairs on the English or Spanish stages in the time of Elizabeth I.) So it was by a jugglery with time that the middle classes devitalized the theatre. When you emphasize *place* in the theatre, you drag down and limit and harness time to it. You thrust the action back into past time, whereas it is precisely the glory of the stage that it is always "now" there. Under such production methods the characters are all dead before the action starts. You don't have to pay deeply from your heart's participation. No great age in the theatre ever attempted to capture the audience's belief through this kind of specification and localization. I became dissatisfied with the theatre because I was unable to lend credence to such childish attempts to be "real."

THE TORCH RACE

I began writing one-act plays that tried to capture not verisimilitude but reality. In *The Happy Journey to Trenton and Camden* four kitchen chairs represent an automobile and a family travels seventy miles in twenty minutes. Ninety years go by in *The Long Christmas Dinner.* In *Pullman Car Hiawatha* some more plain chairs serve as berths and we hear the very vital statistics of the towns and fields that passengers are traversing; we hear their thoughts; we even hear the planets over their heads. In Chinese drama a character, by straddling a stick, conveys to us that he is on horseback. In almost every No play of the Japanese an actor makes a tour of the stage and we know that he is making a long journey. Think of the ubiquity that Shakespeare's stage afforded for the battle scenes at the close of *Julius Caesar* and *Antony and Cleopatra.* As we see them today what a cutting and hacking of the text takes place—what condescension, what contempt for his dramaturgy.

Our Town is not offered as a picture of life in a New Hampshire village; or as a speculation about the conditions of life after death (that element I merely took from Dante's

Purgatory). It is an attempt to find a value above all price for the smallest events in our daily life. I have made the claim as preposterous as possible, for I have set the village against the largest dimensions of time and place. The recurrent words in this play (few have noticed it) are "hundreds," "thousands," and "millions." Emily's joys and griefs, her algebra lessons and her birthday presents—what are they when we consider all the billions of girls who have lived, who are living, and who will live? Each individual's assertion to an absolute reality can only be inner, very inner. And here the method of staging finds its justification—in the first two acts there are at least a few chairs and tables; but when she revisits the earth and the kitchen to which she descended on her twelfth birthday, the very chairs and table are gone. Our claim, our hope, our despair are in the mind—not in things, not in "scenery." Molière said that for the theatre all he needed was a platform and a passion or two. The climax of this play needs only five square feet of boarding and the passion to know what life means to us.

The Matchmaker is an only slightly modified version of *The Merchant of Yonkers* which I wrote in the year after I had written *Our Town*. One way to shake off the nonsense of the nineteenth-century staging is to make fun of it. This play parodies the stock company plays that I used to see at Ye Liberty Theatre, Oakland, California, when I was a boy. I have already read small theses in German comparing it with the great Austrian original on which it is based. The scholars are very bewildered. There's most of the plot (except that our friend Dolly Levi is not in Nestroy's play); there are some of the tags; but it's all "about" quite different matters. Nestroy's wonderful and sardonic plays are—like most of Molière's and Goldoni's—"about" the havoc that people create in their own lives and in those about them through the wrong-headed illusions they cherish. My play is about the aspirations of the young (and not only of the young) for a fuller, freer participation in life. Imagine an Austrian pharmacist going to the shelf to draw from a bottle which he knows to contain a stinging corrosive liquid, guaranteed to remove warts and wens; and imagine his surprise when he discovers that it has been filled with very American birchbark beer.

The Skin of Our Teeth begins, also, by making fun of old-fashioned playwriting; but the audience soon perceives that he is seeing "two times at once." The Antrobus family is living both in prehistoric times and in a New Jersey commuter's suburb today. Again the events of our homely daily life—this time the family life—are depicted against the vast dimensions of time and place. It was written on the eve of our entrance into the war and under strong emotion, and I think it mostly comes alive under conditions of crisis. It has been often charged with being a bookish fantasia about history, full of rather bloodless schoolmasterish jokes. But to have seen it in Germany soon after the war, in the shattered churches and beer halls that were serving as theatres, with audiences whose price of admission meant the loss of a meal and for whom it was of absorbing interest that there was a "recipe for grass soup that did not cause diarrhea," was an experience that was not so cool. I am very proud that this year it has received a first and overwhelming reception in Warsaw.

The play is deeply indebted to James Joyce's *Finnegans Wake*. I should be very happy if, in the future, some author should feel similarly indebted to any work of mine. Literature has always more resembled a torch race than a furious dispute among heirs.

The theatre has lagged behind the other arts in finding the "new ways" to express how men and women think and feel in our time. I am not one of the dramatists we are looking for. I wish I were. I hope I have played a part in preparing the way for them. I am not an innovator but a rediscoverer of forgotten goods and I hope a remover of obtrusive bric-a-brac. And as I view the work of my contemporaries I seem to feel that I am exceptional in one thing—I give (don't I?) the impression of having enormously enjoyed it?

Wilder's Use of Staging

Allan Lewis

Allan Lewis, author of *The Contemporary Theatre*, reports that Wilder once "recalled longingly the time when, at the first performance of Euripides' *Medea*, 'strong men fainted and several children were prematurely born.'" In this essay from his book *American Plays and Playwrights of the Contemporary Theatre*, Lewis examines how Wilder has used very different forms of staging in his various plays in his attempt to restore theater to a commanding role in society. While neither the bare sets of *Our Town* nor the exuberant displays of choreography, song, and costume of the musical *Hello, Dolly!* are likely to make strong men faint, in each case the trappings (or lack thereof) deliberately fit—and enhance—the message of the individual play.

Thornton Wilder and William Saroyan are grouped together as prophets of optimism, a rare commodity in the serious theatre of today. Though ordinarily one would hardly pair the quiet dignity of Wilder with the undisciplined rebellion of Saroyan, the two playwrights are alike in an affirmative response to life. Neither has been too active in the theatre of the past decade, but the first signs of an upswing against the theatre of negativism have given new impetus to revivals of their plays and to a reconsideration of their influence. Both write of simple human beings surrounded by the mystery and enjoyment of life. Saroyan is more instinctive, responding on the immediate emotional level. Wilder coats his small-town folk with philosophic overtones. Both come close to the sermon of a Unitarian minister who has had his fling in Greenwich Village. They seek to break with the "box set" of conventional realism, and are unabashed at giving full lyric expression to the homespun message of heartwarming faith in man.

Wilder is the more careful craftsman, planned and deliberate. After painful analysis, he arrives at the awe and wonder of the simple things in life. Saroyan is reckless and impulsive and responds to life's beauty instinctively. Wilder revises painstakingly: "I constantly rewrite, discard, and replace. . . . There are no first drafts in my life. An incinerator is a writer's best friend."[1] Saroyan appeared on a motion picture set in London with the first line of a screen play and informed those present that the rest of the story would unfold from combined improvisation, while they were shooting. Wilder is the leisured writer with financial means for intellectual detachment; Saroyan is headline sensationalism, dissipating energies and money—yet both have consistently refused to conform to the demands of the commercial theatre.

AN ACTIVE DECADE IN THE THEATRE

In the theatre, Wilder has been the more active in the past decade. *Plays for Bleecker Street* was presented at the Circle in the Square Theatre in 1962. Only the first three of a projected series of fourteen one-act plays were offered by the off-Broadway Bleecker Street Theatre, for which they were expressly written. *Hello, Dolly!* (a musical play based on Wilder's *The Matchmaker*) was the outstanding box-office success of the 1963 season and gives every indication of equaling the sustained record of *My Fair Lady. A Life in the Sun,* based on the Alcestis legend, was performed at the Edinburgh Festival in 1955, was retitled *The Alcestiad,* and then became the libretto for an opera by Louise Talma, produced in Frankfurt in 1962. Paul Hindemith wrote the music for *The Long Christmas Dinner,* which Wilder revised for the premiere in Mannheim in 1961. Leonard Bernstein, composer and director of the New York Philharmonic Society, has indicated his interest in writing the score for a musical play of *The Skin of Our Teeth.*

Wilder's reputation was first earned as a novelist with *The Cabala* (1925), *The Bridge of San Luis Rey* (1927), and *The Woman of Andros* (1930). He has written only four full-length plays: *Our Town, The Skin of Our Teeth,* and *The Matchmaker* (*The Alcestiad* is still unpublished and unperformed in this country). Like many European writers, particularly the French and the Russian, he turns to the theatre for an immediate relationship with audiences and for a

1. *New York Times,* November 6, 1961

definitive summation of his philosophy in human terms. His admiration for the theatre is based on his belief that

> in the great ages it carried on its shoulders the livest realiza-
> tion of public consciousness. The tragic and comic poets of
> Greece, Lope de Vega, Corneille, Racine, Shakespeare, were
> recognized by their contemporaries as expressing what every
> citizen felt dimly and rejoiced to hear concretely.[2]

The theatre should stir the passions and direct the mind. In a recent interview Wilder recalled longingly the time when, at the first performance of Euripides' *Medea,* "strong men fainted and several children were prematurely born." The theatre can be restored to its commanding position if it pursues its role as a critic of society and becomes "the art form by which a nation recognizes its greatness."[3]

OUR TOWN

Our Town, first produced in 1938, achieved this mission. It has come to be considered the most typically American play—a classic of our time. The plot need not be repeated, for the play is known to every high school student, performed by every community theatre, and regarded as an essential element in the repertory of most professional groups. It is a miracle of theatrical magic. By eliminating the usual techniques of realistic representation, and avoiding all pretense, greater illusion was achieved. Wilder is interested in people and ideas, in "reality not verisimilitude." He merged form and meaning in a rare example of artistic unity.

The absence of scenery and elaborate costumes or props, other than a few chairs, a stepladder, and similar simple physical devices, may invite production by budget-conscious producers, but Wilder regards the physical accessories as the least necessary of the theatre's demands. The inner reality of each individual is unique, and imagination is preferable to mechanical devices to achieve it. "Our claim, our hope, our despair are in the mind, not in things, not in scenery," he wrote in the preface to his published plays, and insisted that since the play is a parable of modern times, the language which conveys the meaning should be "heard, not diverted." Such statements by any playwright are usually more theory than fact. *Our Town* appeals to the eye as well as to the ear, and audiences are amused by the bare upstage brick wall.

2. *Ibid.* 3. *Ibid.*

Wilder substitutes a different "scenery"; in *The Skin of Our Teeth* it becomes elaborate at times. Brecht was equally anxious to put an end to the Belasco era, but he used the complementary theatre arts for his purpose, to overwhelm through multiple sense appeals—music as well as words, props as well as costumes, reading as well as hearing. Wilder is likewise not recounting an anecdote or telling a story, which proscenium stage encourages. The unencumbered set reaches into "the truth operative in everyone. The less seen the more heard."

Wilder's departure from the staging of the well-made play was not original. He knew the work of Pirandello and the German expressionists. He had translated André Obey's L*e Viol de Lucrèce,* and *The Merchant of Yonkers* (later *The Matchmaker)* was an adaptation of a work by the nineteenth-century Viennese playwright, Johann Nestroy. More influential, perhaps, was his admiration for the Oriental theatre, which he knew well from his many years in the Far East when his father served in the diplomatic corps. A platform and a passion were the only indispensable ingredients; reducing the theatre to its skeletal requirements made it free to reach beyond the immediate. But no recital of influences can diminish Wilder's originality. All writers take from others. Wilder was skillful enough to add new touches, which, in turn, were seized upon by his European contemporaries—Brecht, Duerrenmatt, and Max Frisch in particular. His techniques made a deeper impression abroad; his story received wider acceptance in his own country.

The Stage Manager, who acts as narrator, commentator, and judge and participates in the action in several roles, is a genial creation. It is he who unites the play, disarms the audience, speaks for the author, and breaks the limitations of time and space. He is Greek chorus, Laudisi of Pirandello's *Six Characters in Search of an Author,* the poet in many guises of Strindberg's *Dream Play,* and Thornton Wilder. Narrators have been used with increasing frequency ever since, as in *The Glass Menagerie, After the Fall,* and *The Ballad of the Sad Cafe.*

Our Town summarizes the totality of life in a small New England village. The first act is labeled "Daily Life"; the second, "Love and Marriage"; the third, obviously, "Death." Grover's Corners is a community set against all of time. The characters are not specific individuals, psychologically revealed, but types. The Webbs and the Gibbses are representative of American middle-class life. Emily and George are young boy and young girl. They have already become legendary, ingrained in the myths of a nation. The method Wilder employs is quickly apparent. The smallest daily chores, the most repeated of living action, the local events—doing homework, listening to the Albany train, watching the boy down at the stable, ironing a dress—are magnified to equality with the movement of the stars. Whatever *is,* belongs to an intricately connected and meaningful system. Just as the earth is a speck in an endless succession of planetary units, so each moment of breathing is part of the history of man. Timelessness and pancakes are discussed in the same everyday language.

Most of the scenes could be inserted into a realistic play. Even the dead talk as though they were gathered around a New Hampshire cracker barrel. Pain and suffering are tolerable, for what we endure is both unique and common to all. Emily's early death in childbirth touches our hearts, but she is still with us in death. Her final statement is the lesson we never learn:

> We don't have time to look at one another . . . Oh earth, you're too wonderful for anyone to realize you . . . Do any human beings ever realize life while they live it—every, every minute?

Simon Stimson, the local drunk, now with the deceased, answers:

> That's what it was to be alive . . . to spend and to waste time, as though you had a million years.

Middle-class life is given dignity by relating it to the cosmos. Wilder objected to the theatre which arose in the nineteenth century with the domination of the merchant. "They wanted their theater soothing . . . they distrusted the passions and tried to deny them." The rules that developed for the situation play which did not disturb deprived the theatre of vitality. Wilder, resenting middle-class domination, broke all the rules and wrote the most complete middle-class play.

THE SKIN OF OUR TEETH

The Skin of Our Teeth uses the same technique, but carries it to the logical conclusion of relating the seemingly unimportant to the grandiose. Mr. and Mrs. Antrobus, of Excelsior, New Jersey, are Adam and Eve, Renaissance figures, and also the suburban neighbors next door. All history is merged with the present, picturing the rise from primordial ignorance to the continuing problem of survival. In the first act, man is pitted against the destructive forces of nature. The audience is called upon to help, Prometheus-like, by passing up chairs to keep the home fires burning during the glacial age. In the second act, man is ranged against the moral order, and in the third, against himself. A typical American family is the Human Family. The allegory borders upon the fantastic and the incredible—Mr. Antrobus' arrival on time at his office is as important as the invention of the wheel and the alphabet.

Wilder's use of composite historical characters was similar to that in *Finnegans Wake*. He had lectured on the work of James Joyce at the University of Chicago, and was taken to task for not indicating his sources. Wilder dismissed the charges by adding to the preface of the published version of the play:

> I should be very happy if, in the future, some author should feel similarly indebted to any work of mine. Literature has always more resembled a torch race, than a furious dispute among heirs.

The play is a brilliant example of expressionistic theatre. Unities of place and action are abolished. Man's fate is compressed into a circus satire in which burlesque and vaudeville antics combine with tightrope-walking on the razor edge of despair. Like Max Frisch in *The Chinese Wall* and Bertolt Brecht in *Mother Courage,* Wilder indicates that man has learned little from experience, but must go on laughing and striving. He cannot renege now and permit chaos to triumph. Somehow or other, he will survive. At the end of the play, when Antrobus has lost "the most important thing of all: the desire to begin again, to start building," Sabina, who is Vice and Virtue, Sex and Self-interest, Love and Deception, admonishes him, as she prepares to go to the movies, that she will work with him if he has any ideas about "improving the crazy old world." Antrobus adds:

> I've never forgotten for long at a time that living is struggle . . . all I ask is the chance to build new worlds and God has always given us that . . . we've come a long way.

As Sabina comes downstage to tell the audience good-night, she reassures all that as far as Mr. and Mrs. Antrobus are concerned, "their heads are full of plans and they are as confident as the first day they began."

Though hailed in Europe, the play had a mixed reception in New York. Many regarded it as a silly extravaganza, a sophomoric lampoon of history. Brooks Atkinson was enthusiastic, terming it "one of the wisest and friskiest comedies." The play won for Wilder his third Pulitzer Prize, his second for a dramatic work. It ranks with the best of Brecht—an example of historical realism in which the accumulation of evidence permits audiences to pass judgment.

THE MERCHANT OF YONKERS/ THE MATCHMAKER/HELLO, DOLLY!

The Merchant of Yonkers was Wilder's only failure, despite the fanfare that attended a production by Max Reinhardt, with an all-star cast headed by Jane Cowl and June Walker. Wilder refused to let the material die. He was determined to pull it through to survival, in the manner of Antrobus with mankind. Rewritten as *The Matchmaker* and directed by Tyrone Guthrie, the play did prove a success sixteen years later. The retired and professorial Wilder had become the maverick with three consecutive triumphs.

A libretto by Michael Stewart and music and lyrics by Jerry Hyman transformed *The Matchmaker* into *Hello, Dolly!*—the outstanding musical play of the 1964 season. The production was a triumph of the theatre arts, a vindication of the major trend in musical theatre. Choreography, costumes, design, and songs were interrelated with plot. Gower Champion, the director, exercised an overall control that fashioned a unified experience in the tradition of *Oklahoma!* Wilder's play gained in the process. As an acted piece, it was handicapped by reliance on verbal appeal. The musical version gave fuller scope than Wilder's original prose to the joyous sensation of being alive. The appeal to the eye, which Wilder had discounted, the multiple appeal to the ear, the evocation of unheard songs, enhanced a mediocre work and achieved a refreshing reiteration of "Isn't the world full of such wonderful things?" Sentimental and nostalgic, *Hello, Dolly!* restates the trite maxims that love conquers all, that woman is the greatest work of God, and that money is good only when it becomes "manure to be spread around to help young things grow." Despite Wilder's efforts to convert the middle-class theatre from its devotion to the soporific and its ignoring of the

> questions about the nature of life which seem to be sufficiently answered by the demonstration of financial status and by conformity to some clearly established rules of decorum,

the hit musical inspired by Wilder's work is a *soothing* play.

WILDER'S AMAZING THEATRICAL GIFT

This raises the question of Thornton Wilder's amazing gift. He deals with the most commonplace, the most trivial, relationships and gives the impression of being exceedingly profound. Remove the deceptive overtones, and his work all winds up with a simplistic philosophy—live every moment of your life, for life is beautiful; the tragedy is human wastefulness. Such nostrums, as in the case of Saroyan, fall short of revelation. The arts of the theatre, skillfully employed, can cover dross with an alluring sheen.

A defense of Wilder can be based on his similarity with Camus. Both explore consciously the absurdity of man's plight, reject irrational remedies, and end by asserting that at least one can live by not adding to the suffering of mankind. Both recognize the anxieties that plague the world, but rather than welcome defeat, they rely on man to effect solutions as he always has. Optimism is better conveyed in song and dance. *Hello, Dolly!* may be Wilder's most explicit statement.

PLAYS FOR BLEECKER STREET

Plays for Bleecker Street is an attempt to express in dramatic terms a definitive summary of Wilder's beliefs. The cycle of one-act plays will constitute a morality of the twentieth century. The theatre, Wilder feels, can be strengthened to achieve its role as the "signature of an age."

The overall title, *Plays for Bleecker Street,* is added proof of Wilder's opposition to the picture-frame stage, which "militates against belief" and squeezes the drama into a "removed showcase." A precondition for a revitalized theatre is to "kick the proscenium down." Wilder enjoys reminding us that in the great theatre of the past the audience encircled the acting area on three sides. The plays were entrusted to the Circle in the Square Theatre, a pioneer in the growing arena theatre movement. Though Wilder can afford artistic independence, his action was a courageous defiance of Broadway commercialism and its reluctance to experiment. He gave a boost to the struggling little theatres of New York by proving his willingness to have his work seen first at a small, off-Broadway organization.

The cycle consists of two series of seven plays each, entitled respectively *The Seven Ages of Man* and *The Seven Deadly Sins.* The first will be for five actors, the second for four. Eventually, when completed, all fourteen will be presented in sequence on several successive evenings in the theatre. The only ones available so far are *Infancy* and *Childhood*, the first two of *The Seven Ages of Man*, and *Someone from Assisi* or *Lust*, number four of *The Seven Deadly Sins*.

Infancy deals with two children in perambulators being taken for a walk by their parents. The parts of the children are played by grown actors dressed in baby clothes, who comment on the world situation, the adult world, and their own growing pains. Their highly imaginative response to their environment is reminiscent of Wordsworth's "The child is father to the man." *Childhood* reveals the gulf that separates the inner worlds of children and adults, no matter how wholesome and loving their relationship may be. In both plays, the child's struggle for improvement is thwarted by those who are older. "The reason why the world is in such a sloppy state," Wilder has remarked, "is that our parents were so stupid." The third of the plays deals with a fictionalized incident in the life of St. Francis of Assisi, when he was seized with desire for the beautiful Mona Lucrezia.

On the basis of but three examples of a large undertaking, judgment can be only tentative. *Infancy* is in the gay mood of *The Skin of Our Teeth*, and is by far the most effective on stage. *Someone from Assisi* is a disappointment. It lacks purpose and gives the impression of being removed from context. It is a serious sermon about the nature of lust, and Wilder is much more comfortable in the comic vein. The total concept of the cycle, however, is on a grand scale—the use of the theatre to crystallize views about "our lives and errors" from birth to death.

> I am interested in the drives that operate in society and in every man. Pride, avarice, and envy are in every home. I am not interested in the ephemeral—such subjects as the adulteries of dentists. I am interested in those things that repeat and repeat in the lives of millions.[4]

With this statement, Thornton Wilder, at seventy, becomes the youngest of our playwrights.

4. ibid.

An Unfashionable Optimist

Gerald Weales

Gerald Weales is an author and editor of several books on drama and film including *American Drama Since World War II, Religion in Modern English Drama,* and *Canned Goods as Caviar: American Film Comedy of the 1930s.* In this selection, Weales contends that Thornton Wilder's work presents a refreshing optimism. Most "serious" playwrights place the dignity of man well in the background of their darker subjects, Weales comments, and seem to feel it is more intellectually profound to be despairing than sunny. Wilder has shown the courage to be upbeat. Even his minimal stage sets reflect his belief that human reality is a quality of the mind, Weales points out, not dependent on "realistic" staging.

Thornton Wilder's recently issued *Three Plays* might have been called *The Collected Plays.* Except for two early books of short plays, the unpublished *A Life in the Sun* and the new one-acters that are presumably scheduled for production at the Circle in the Square,[1] the three plays—*Our Town, The Skin of Our Teeth* and *The Matchmaker*—comprise the bulk of Wilder's work for the theater. In the introduction to his first book of short plays, *The Angel That Troubled the Waters* (1928), Wilder spoke of "the inertia that barely permits me to write." Whether because of that inertia or a fondness for tinkering with already completed works (*Our Town* grew out of two early one-acters; *The Matchmaker* is a revision of a 1939 play, *The Merchant of Yonkers*), his theatrical output is small. Yet, he is one of America's most important playwrights.

Playwrights have a way of marking their work with the signature of personal mannerisms. A play of Tennessee

1. an off-Broadway theater in New York City

Williams or Eugene O'Neill, for instance, is easily identifiable. Wilder's three plays, unmistakably his, are dissimilar on the surface—one an essay in regionless regionalism, one an expressionistic comedy, one a traditional farce. In their manner they share only a distaste for conventional naturalistic staging; it is their matter that points an insistent finger at the author. Each of the plays embodies Wilder's concern with, admiration for and love of human life at its most ordinary, which is, for him, at its most consistent preoccupation with love, death, laughter, boredom, aspiration and despair.

An Optimist by Instinct

Malcolm Cowley, in his introduction to *A Thornton Wilder Trio,* the re-issue of Wilder's first three novels, wrote, "He is optimistic by instinct, in the fashion of an older America." One of the remarkable things about Wilder's plays is that they—like his novels—have declared his optimism with a directness that is unusual on the American stage, at least among serious playwrights. The dignity of man is apparent behind the cosmic and familiar sufferings of O'Neill and behind the political and social uncertainty of Clifford Odets and Arthur Miller, perhaps even behind the sexual nervousness of Tennessee Williams, but in Wilder it is in the foreground. The emphasis, however, is not so much on dignity as it is on man; the one implies the other. Nor is his optimism the kind of adolescent enthusiasm that seems to be the stuff of William Saroyan's plays (Saroyan's cry of love, love, love has become so shrill that one suspects that he has not yet convinced himself); it is a recognition that pain, cruelty, death and failure are part of living, but that they can never completely define life. All of Wilder's plays say, with Chrysis in his novel *The Woman of Andros,* "that I have known the worst that the world can do to me, and that nevertheless I praise the world and all living."

There is an uncomfortable attitude around today that the clichés of despair are more profound than the bromides of optimism; it is intellectually proper to talk about the dark night of the soul, but only a popular song would be willing to walk on the sunny side of the street. Every man must decide whether he is a "lone, lorn creetur" with Mrs. Gummidge or whether, like Mr. Micawber, he lives on the expectation that something is about to turn up. At the moment the vote seems to be with Mrs. Gummidge, and Wilder's reputation has suffered as a result. People talk of outgrowing Wilder, as they talk of outgrowing Shaw, but they mean simply that even if one does believe in the ultimate value of human life, one does not say so, except obliquely. Wilder once told a reporter from *Time*, "Literature is the orchestration of platitudes." Wilder has chosen the unfashionable platitudes of the optimist; he has repeated them in his plays even though he knows, like Captain Alvarado in *The Bridge of San Luis Rey*, that "there are times when it requires a high courage to speak the banal." It is his distinction as a playwright that banality emerges as—what it is—one kind of truth.

A PASSION FOR LIFE—AND TO LEARN WHAT LIFE MEANS

All three of Wilder's plays grow out of "the passion to know what life means to us." *Our Town* is an "attempt to find a value above all price for the smallest events in our daily life." The play is concerned, for the most part, with the ritual of daily tasks; the major actions in the play (Emily Webb's marriage to George Gibbs and her death in childbirth) celebrate those basic commonplaces that Sweeney expected to find on his cannibal isle: "Birth, and copulation, and death." Each of the events, the ordinary and the special (which is special only to Emily and George and those close to them), is seen as part of a continuing stream of life from which it grows and into which it will be absorbed and finally forgotten. The play is, in one sense, antitheatrical; instead of enlarging a moment until it bursts, throwing its significance into the audience, it cherishes the small and the everyday (whether it be cooking breakfast or dying). If the perspective is long enough, the individual and the general become one. For one kind of mind, such a long view might reduce life to inconsequence; for Wilder, it gives to the simplest action and the simplest emotion not cosmic value (the dead forget), but human value.

As *Our Town* is a play about the significance of the routine of living, so *The Matchmaker* is about man's attempt to dress that routine in the fantastic and the exciting; it is, as Barnaby says in his curtain speech, "about adventure." Adapted from a nineteenth century German farce, which was in turn taken from an English source, the play makes happy use of a stageful of stock farcical situations and devices. There is an elopement that must wait for parental (here, avuncular) approval. There are two innocent young men, loose in the wicked city. There are mistaken identities, assumed names, disguises. There is the final gathering and forgiving of all the erring characters in the play, an occasion for three marriages and a healthy helping of material and spiritual rewards. Picking its way among the farcical furniture of the play is Wilder's theme, the insistence that life cannot be embraced with care and hedging. "Is this an adventure?" asks Barnaby in Act Two, and Cornelius answers, "No, but it may be." Dolly Levi, the matchmaker, Wilder's wonderful addition to the German play, elbows her way through the action, like an edited echo of Cornelius' words: it not only may be, it can be, it must be. "My play," says Wilder, "is about the aspirations of the young (and not only of the young) for a fuller, freer participation in life."

The Skin of Our Teeth is Wilder's best play and his most ambitious one. It is a history of man under crisis. In Act One, the Antrobus family survive the ice age; in Act Two, they escape the deluge; in Act Three, they live through a world war. After each near destruction, Antrobus—falling back always on the words of the great prophets, thinkers and poets—begins to build again. The power of the play lies in the four main characters—Mr. and Mrs. Antrobus, their son Henry, and the maid-mistress Lily-Sabina. Antrobus is man, the creator (in the play he invents the wheel and the alphabet), and Henry (Cain) is man, the destroyer. These two are not only at war with one another; each is at war within himself. Antrobus' enthusiasm drains off easily into despair and his mind readily wanders from the alphabet to the maid; Henry not only wants to destroy his family, he wants to join it. Mrs. Antrobus and Sabina also form a contrast, that between Eve and Lilith, between woman as wife, mother and home-builder and woman as sexual object and home-wrecker. The play is often broadly funny, often sidetracked by its delight in intellectual jokes, but the warring qualities that go to make up man are always in evidence in the four characters, who, with the daughter Gladys (on hand to have a baby in Act Three), must be saved together if they are to be saved at all. The family, including Henry-Cain, always comes through; man is saved by the skin of his teeth, but with his evil as well as his aspirations intact.

UNCONVENTIONAL STAGING

All of Wilder's plays avoid conventional staging. They either attack it head-on, using the weapons of expressionism, as in

Our Town and *The Skin of Our Teeth,* or they join it with a
vengeance, as in *The Matchmaker,* and try to laugh it off the
stage. His attempt to splinter the box-set [proscenium stage,
which separates the audience from the play] or to treat it as
though it were a farceur's mask (the fight was pretty well
won when he got into it) grew out of his belief that plays
begin in generalization; the correct teacups on the correct
table in the correct drawing room have a way of reducing
universals to the tiresomely specific. Even in his novels, as
Cowley has pointed out, the settings are relatively unimportant. He is concerned with the recurrent human predica-
ments at the expense of the immediate surroundings. *The
Skin of Our Teeth* brings the ice age, Noah's flood, the invention of the wheel and Homer (singing "Jingle Bells") to contemporary New Jersey; *Our Town* can be identified as
Grover's Corners, New Hampshire, but it is also to be our
town wherever and at whatever time we live, as Editor Webb
implies when he says of ancient Babylon, "every night all
those families sat down to supper, and the father came home
from his work, and the smoke went up the chimney,—same
as here." The immediate references for the characters of *The
Matchmaker* are the stock figures of farce—the irate father,
the reluctant maiden, the drunken servant, the interfering
vice. The strength of the play lies, however, in the fact that,
even while they retain the force of philosophical generalization, the characters and the situations take on dramatic individuality; audiences identify with individuals not with
abstractions.

For all its importance to the themes of the plays, Wilder's
non-naturalistic structure gives too easy entrance to his
chief dramatic fault, a tendency to be overly didactic. He
seems afraid that apparent points will be missed. The stage
manager in *Our Town* explains too much and points up too
many morals. The long asides in *The Matchmaker* (although
I admire Mrs. Levi's, as Ruth Gordon read it) too often do
what the action has already done. The most obvious example is the emergency rehearsal at the beginning of Act Three
of *The Skin of Our Teeth;* although there are funny things in
it and although it is there, too, to emphasize Wilder's belief
that human reality is a quality of the mind and not the result
of realistic staging, it sounds as though the author were half-
afraid that the audience would not understand the passing of
the hours that speak the words of the philosophers. These

are minor blemishes, however; they weaken the plays without undermining them.

Wilder, as he says in his introduction, is not an innovator. He is not the kind of playwright who gathers disciples or inspires copyists. He is simply a man who has gone his own way, finding or borrowing the forms in which he could say what was on his mind. He has published only three full-length plays, but they are all good plays and that—on the American stage, or any stage—is an achievement.

CHAPTER 3

Pulitzer #1: *The Bridge of San Luis Rey*

The Factual People and Places Behind *The Bridge of San Luis Rey*

Linda Simon

The Bridge of San Luis Rey is based on the collapse of an actual bridge in Peru, writes Linda Simon, and several of the main characters were drawn from people Wilder knew. These real-world influences are all pulled into the service of what she calls "the literary enthusiasms and personal obsessions that occupied Thornton at the time." No less than Brother Juniper, the Franciscan friar who studies the lives of the victims to find God's hand at work, Wilder is curious to know whether those who died in the bridge's collapse were victims of destiny or circumstance. But despite Brother Juniper's convictions, Simon notes, Wilder's own conclusions are ambiguous. Linda Simon is the author of *The Biography of Alice B. Toklas* and editor of *Gertrude Stein: A Composite Portrait.*

"I write first as if I were writing about people we know," Thornton Wilder once said. "Then I do my research after I write—not before."[1] The basis for *The Bridge* was not so much in historical research as it was in the literary enthusiasms and personal obsessions that occupied Wilder at the time. But of course there was a kernel of historical fact in his tale. There had been a bridge, described as being "two hundred paces" long, made of cables hand-twisted from the fibers of the maguey plant. In heavy wind, it swung frighteningly over a dark abyss, above threatening waves that thundered against the rocks. It had been built across the Apurímac River in Peru in about 1350 and had lasted for hundreds of years, support-

1. Boston *Traveler*, December 14, 1955

ed on either side by stone pillars. It was a much used thoroughfare, and every two years the cables were renewed and the wood planking replaced. But when the wheel came into common use among the Indian population, the bridge was allowed slowly to decay. It collapsed, and the few travelers upon it were plunged to their death.

Like many before him, Wilder asked, "Why? Why were those particular travelers chosen to die? Or were they chosen at all?" But his questions came from another source as well, a passage from the Bible [Luke 13:4] that continually rang in his mind:

> Or those eighteen, upon whom the tower in Siloam fell, and slew them, think ye that they were sinners above all men that dwelt in Jerusalem?

The passage set the theme; the characters were drawn from many sources.

The book is divided into five parts, with the central three describing the lives of the victims: the Marquesa de Montemayor and her servant Pepita, Esteban, Uncle Pio, and a young boy, Don Jaime. It is the self-imposed task of a Franciscan monk, Brother Juniper, to investigate their deaths and determine if "we live by accident and die by accident, or we live by plan and die by plan." For Brother Juniper there is no doubt: the accident must have been an act of God, and therefore the life and death of each person involved must have some meaning.

THE MARQUESA AND PEPITA

He tells us first about Doña María, the Marquesa de Montemayor, known through legend and her letters to her daughter. Doña Maria was inspired by Wilder's fascination for Madame de Sévigné, an enthusiasm he could not fully explain. "She is not devastatingly witty nor wise," he admitted once. "She is simply at one with French syntax."[2] So, too, the Marquesa frequently blunders in her dealings with others, but her letters are full of unleashed passion and "flamboyant" language. Doña María, like Wilder's early St. Zabett, rebels against marriage. But she is forced into a mismatched union by her mother and eventually has a daughter, the haughty Doña Clara. Doña María suffers unrequited love for

2. Richard Goldstone, "Thornton Wilder," in Malcolm Cowley, ed., *Writers at Work*, p. 108

her daughter, and her suffering gives her insight into the isolation of other humans. "She saw that the people of this world moved about in an armour of egotism, drunk with self-gazing, a thirst for compliments, hearing little of what was said to them, unmoved by accidents that befell their closest friends, in dread of all appeals that might interrupt their long communion with their own desires." Yet she, too, becomes blind to love and fails to appreciate the singular spirit of her young maid, Pepita, who despite her unhappiness serves her mistress in good faith.

Contrasted with the Marquesa is an Abbess, Madre María del Pilar, loosely modeled on Wilder's aunt Charlotte, his father's sister, then chairman of the International Committee of the YWCA and a woman Wilder admired and respected. The Abbess is an ardent feminist who wants only "to attach a little dignity to women." She realizes, of course, the futility of her goal in eighteenth-century Peru. Yet like a swallow who tried to build a mountain by adding a single pebble to a pile every thousand years, the Abbess perseveres. She sends her protégé, Pepita, to the Marquesa because she knows that not even the suffocating existence of that life will damp the girl's spirit.

Indeed, it is Pepita who ultimately shows Doña María that her life spent in pursuit of her daughter's affections has been wasted; Doña María realizes that she was a coward in both living and loving and resolves to start anew. "'Let me live now,' she whispered. 'Let me begin again.'" But two days later, she and Pepita die crossing the bridge.

ESTEBAN AND MANUEL

The characters in the next section are closer to Wilder's own life. Esteban and Manuel are orphaned twins, raised by the Abbess, who, despite her generalized hatred of men, grew fond of the two boys. The duality of personalities is treated more emotionally here than it was in *The Cabala*, where Samuele and James Blair are contrasted. For Wilder, the idea of being a twin, of living with a double, was almost an obsession.[3] His dead brother often haunted him; he carried within him the image of an identical likeness.

Esteban and Manuel are so close in spirit that "love is inadequate to describe their profound identity with one

---

3. Thornton Wilder's twin brother died within hours of birth.

another." They invent their own language and find that telepathy often occurs between them. No matter what they do or where they go, they are certain of one thing: "All the world was remote and strange and hostile except one's brother."

But their bond is broken when Manuel becomes infatuated with a beautiful actress, known as the Perichole. His brother feels estranged and once threatens to leave. There is a crisis, however: Manuel cuts his knee and is badly wounded. Esteban nurses him, but the infection worsens and his brother becomes delirious. Suddenly he begins to curse Esteban for coming between him and the actress. For several nights Esteban suffers under his brother's raving; on the third night, Manuel dies.

Esteban's grief causes near-madness. At first he pretends to be Manuel, and no one is the wiser. But he meets a sagacious sea captain, Alvarado, to whom he tells the truth, and his confession seems to relieve him somewhat. Alvarado invites him to join his crew. Esteban agrees, provided he can take on the hardest work. He knows suicide is proscribed, he tells Alvarado, but clearly he is seeking death in life.

Just before sailing, however, Esteban changes his mind, vacillates, and tries to kill himself. He cannot bear to leave Peru. He cannot bear to live alone. Alvarado tries to comfort him, but he knows how meaningless his words must sound to the young man. "We do what we can," he tells him. "We push on, Esteban, as best we can. It isn't for long, you know. Time keeps going by. You'll be surprised at the way time passes." Esteban, calmed, leaves with the captain and is killed when the bridge collapses.

THE PERICHOLE AND UNCLE PIO

The Perichole and her benefactor, Uncle Pio, are met again in the fourth section. Uncle Pio is a sympathetic character, a lonely man who discovered the actress when she was the waif Micaela Villegas and transformed her into an idolized figure. Uncle Pio decides early in his life that he will try to fulfill three aims: independence—keeping emotionally detached from people while able to act as "an agent" in their lives; proximity to beautiful women who would depend on him when they were in trouble, though they would not, he thought, love him; involvement with those who loved Spanish literature and its masterpieces, especially in the theater. His life with the Perichole seems on the surface to fill all three, but gradually it becomes evident that Uncle Pio is hardly detached from the young woman. He realizes that the world may be divided into two groups, "those who had loved and those who had not." His devotion to the actress places him among the former.

Though Uncle Pio's attachment to the Perichole transcends a mentor-student or father-daughter relationship, it never implies sexuality. Instead, Uncle Pio understands the rare communion between the two, and does not want to lose it. When the Perichole retires from the stage and finds a position in Peruvian high society, he urges her to return with him to Madrid and to the theater. But she refuses, mocking his dreams, and turns him away. Uncle Pio does not give up, however. Even when the Perichole contracts smallpox, he tries to see her, and one day comes upon her accidentally unveiled, her scars revealed as she tries to cover them with make-up. Enraged, she throws him out of her house. Still he persists. Finally he implores her to allow him to take her young son and raise him for a year. He will educate the boy as he did her; and the child will be his new companion. She relents and sends her beloved Jaime to Uncle Pio. The next day the two leave for Lima—and cross the bridge.

AMBIGUOUS LESSONS

Despite Brother Juniper's dogged efforts, the author is not convinced that the collapse of the bridge was a deliberate and meaningful act of God. Surely there are lessons to be learned from the close examination of any life, but what these lessons teach are ambiguous. Each in a different way, the victims sought love; each was the victim of love. The dead live in the memory of the living until they, too, die and are forgotten. "But the love will have been enough; all those impulses of love return to the love that made them. Even memory is not necessary for love. There is a land of the living and a land of the dead and the bridge is love, the only survival, the only meaning."

CRITICAL ACCLAIM

Hardly anyone—least of all Wilder—was prepared for the accolades bestowed upon *The Bridge of San Luis Rey* when it appeared in late fall. "A new talent, and a very distinguished one, has appeared in American letters," Lee Wilson Dodd declared in the *Saturday Review*. While *The Cabala* had hinted at promise, Thornton's full talent was not yet evident. "It grows clear with his second book . . . ," Dodd saw,

> that Mr. Thornton Wilder is not just another literate and sophisticated young man. *The Cabala*, his first book, had distinction, passages of genuine insight and beauty; yet there was about it an air of the tentative, the experimental. One felt that Mr. Wilder had wings, that they would prove to be good wings—and even enchanted wings; but one felt, also, that he was merely trying them out a little before they were fully fledged. There was a general atmosphere of flutter eddying round the whole charming performance.

But *The Bridge*, Dodd thought, was "a tale which I am grievously tempted to call a masterpiece. . . . This book is a poem, if you will, a romantic poem—for its true matter is human love."[4]

Wilder was heralded also in *The New Republic*, where Malcolm Cowley found that the book "without pretense to greatness is perfect in itself. . . . In *The Bridge of San Luis Rey*, the texture is completely unified; nothing falls short of its mark; nothing exceeds it; and the book as a whole is like some faultless temple erected to a minor deity."[5]

By the end of the year, praise for the book had appeared in most newspapers and magazines across the country. And in February an important review appeared in London's *Evening Standard*. Arnold Bennett wrote that he had been "dazzled" by the unsurpassed writing in the novel. "The author does not search for the right word. He calls, it comes."[6] Like his fictional Cabalists, Thornton had found that "to wish is to command." Yet he read each review in hope of some instruction, some advice. He wanted to be evaluated, and though he was more than pleased by the praise he was receiving, he was thankful, too, for less favorable assessments.[7] One of these came in March, 1928.

"And Then the (Bridge) Failed" was John Herrmann's review in *transition*, the Paris-based literary journal.

> Now that it is definitely established that *The Bridge of San Luis Rey* by Thornton Wilder is a classic (Burton Rascoe), a work of genius (William Lyon Phelps), a little masterpiece

4. December 3, 1927, p. 371 5. December 28, 1927, p. 173 6. February 28, 1928 7. TW to Henry Blake Fuller, May 12, 1928

and of course a contribution to literature (Isabel Patterson), unsurpassed (Arnold Bennett), a great success for the discriminating (Henry Seidel Canby), and able to refresh such a jaded reviewer as Harry Hansen (Harry Hansen), I will horn in with two fingers and point out that the old bunkum is still the cat's eyebrows.

Herrmann thought the plot was "founded on a trick, a chain of feeble attempts at character sketching." The theme was inconsequential, he went on, and the descriptions "beatific." It would be a best seller only "because there is nothing new about it and readers have gotten used to it." But Herrmann scored the critics for heaping undeserved praise on what was, in his view, a failure.

Fortunately, Herrmann's view was in the minority. . . . On May 7, 1928, [Thornton Wilder] won his first Pulitzer Prize.

The Bridge of San Luis Rey: A Christian Novel

M.C. Kuner

> Although Brother Juniper, the Franciscan friar who
> narrates *The Bridge*, misses the point of God's pur-
> pose, the book is built on Christian themes, declares
> M.C. Kuner, an associate professor of English at
> Hunter College in New York. In this excerpt from her
> book *Thornton Wilder: The Bright and the Dark*, she
> traces such Christian principles as the significance
> of suffering and the acceptance of the will of God. In
> *The Bridge*, Wilder examines every kind of love, she
> notes, but the impure human loves are finally fil-
> tered out to lead the bridge's victims to *agape*, the
> kind of love God has for people.

The Bridge of San Luis Rey can most correctly be character-
ized as a Christian novel in that it deals with themes and
ideas that are part of the Christian faith. For example, what
might be regarded as failure in the eyes of the world may, in
fact, be success in the judgment of God. Suffering, which so
often seems pointless, may have a significance, although we
apprehend it only "through a glass, darkly." Thus Part One
is entitled "Perhaps an Accident"; Part Five, "Perhaps an
Intention." What looks like happenstance may indeed have a
design to it, but one cannot be sure; hence the "perhaps." As
Wilder himself has explained it, it is the "magic unity of purpose and chance, destiny and accident, that I have tried to
describe in my books."

Other traditional Christian themes abound. There is value
in suffering as a means of transforming character and
ennobling it. Not, it must be added, the passive kind that
turns a human being into an unthinking slave, but rather the
willingness to recognize that pain and death are threads in
the tapestry of life. We cannot avoid them, but we can use

them to enrich the pattern of our existence. . . . Wilder stands midway between those writers of the past who accepted their religion more or less unquestioningly ("Whatever is, is right") and those of his own day who relegated faith to the junk-heap of superstition. Perhaps Arthur Koestler, in his novel *The Age of Longing,* summed up the problem best [the italics in the quotation have been added]:

> Some people suffer and become saints. Others, by the same experience, are turned into brutes thirsting for vengeance. Others, just into neurotics. *To draw spiritual nourishment from suffering, one must be endowed with the right kind of digestive system.* Otherwise suffering turns sour on one. It was bad policy on the part of God to inflict suffering indiscriminately. It was like ordering laxatives for every kind of disease.

By and large, the people who most interest Wilder and the characters he most favors in his books are those with "the right kind of digestive system." Possibly it is his concentration on this category of human being (as contrasted, say, with such writers as François Mauriac or Graham Greene, who focus on those who have turned sour) that sometimes makes Wilder's philosophy seem too Pollyana-ish and his work too bland. Certainly the serenity of his point of view is in sharp conflict with the kind of novel that was being written in 1927, an age deeply preoccupied with the "lost generation."

DEATH AND ISOLATION

If suffering, however, is to be seen in its positive aspects, another element must accompany it: resignation, the acceptance of the will of God. Consequently, although death comes to the leading characters of *The Bridge* (in fact, death occupies the foreground of all Wilder's novels and plays), suicide seldom makes its appearance. For death belongs to the natural order of things, whereas suicide, the final act of defiant despair, disturbs the pattern. (Marcantonio of *The Cabala* is one of the few who takes this route.) Although the characters have known despair that has brought them to the brink of self-destruction, when death finds them on the bridge they have overcome their agony and look forward to a new and better life. Having discovered the noblest portion of their natures when they were under stress, they really have, artistically speaking, no further reason to survive. They have fulfilled their destiny.

Because so much of the novel deals with the theme of suffering, it necessarily explores its concomitant, loneliness. All the characters in *The Bridge* are, in one way or another, isolated: from God, from society, from relatives, from friends, from lovers. Even when they are most surrounded by groups of people, they are most conscious of their alienation. The Marquesa is abandoned by her daughter, whom she loves; Esteban and Manuel, twin brothers, are orphans who have neither family nor friends; Pepita, who dies with the Marquesa, is also alone in the world; and Uncle Pio and the little boy, Jaime, have little beyond each other. Like Christ, praying alone in the Garden of Gethsemane, forgotten by disciples who were too tired to keep watch with Him, those on the bridge live out their days forgotten by their fellows. But when they understand and accept the fact that loneliness is the natural condition (in the words of a character in T.S. Eliot's *The Cocktail Party*, "Hell is oneself, Hell is alone, the other figures in it merely projections. . . . One is always alone."), they begin to appreciate their common humanity. And at the same time they learn the name of the only cure for their loneliness—a love that transcends self.

A USEFUL TECHNIQUE FOR SERIOUS THEMES

Though Wilder, when he wrote this novel, was only thirty, he had already developed a technique that was going to prove increasingly useful in giving shape to his major ideas. In such widely divergent future novels as *Heaven's My Destination* and *The Ides of March*, in plays like *Our Town* and *The Skin of Our Teeth*, he simply refines what he is doing in *The Bridge*. The themes in *The Bridge* are serious, transcendental. The content is religious, philosophical. From a practical point of view, these elements are not going to send the average reader rushing to buy the book. So Wilder's style becomes simple, unadorned; more important, he juxtaposes theological problems with everyday activities. For example, he spends some time describing the bridge physically: how well it is built, of what it is made, how proud the people are of its fame. It is quite important as a utilitarian object. We are so lulled by the ordinary, it seems so much part of our own lives, that we look no further. And when we have become comfortable with its familiar things, suddenly they turn into something else and become metaphysical symbols. That is why *Our Town*, which has a great deal to say about abstract subjects, is so convincing in its concentration on detail. And again, in *The Ides of March*, where Wilder raises questions that go far beyond the world of Julius Caesar, he surrounds these questions with the trivia of gossip, domestic intrigue, all the petty considerations of our daily routine had we been Romans. But this is not a mere literary device that Wilder employs to popularize his work: it springs from a belief that is characteristic of his temperament. One's immortal soul and one's laundry *have* to be considered simultaneously.

BROTHER JUNIPER

Like *The Eighth Day*, written forty years later, *The Bridge* opens with a calm recitation of a disaster—the death of five people caused by the collapse of a bridge. Significantly, the day on which it happens is Friday, Passion Day; the time is exactly noon—both hands of the clock pointing up. The faceless narrator tells us that everyone is deeply upset by the tragedy, though he cannot understand why, since people have accepted all sorts of other misfortunes with equanimity: tidal waves, earthquakes, crumbling towers. But there was something different, something special about this bridge, and so a little Franciscan friar, who "accidentally" happened to be in Peru at that time converting the Indians and who has witnessed the misfortune, decides to investigate the reason for it. It is Brother Juniper who initiates the first part, "Perhaps an Accident," for by discovering why those particular five people were the victims he believes he can prove that the universe operates according to a plan. Rather delightfully, Wilder gives us a brief sketch of the little Franciscan, who sees no reason why theology cannot be an exact science, like mathematics. . . .

As he is described, Brother Juniper hardly seems an Italian Catholic: he sounds much more like Wilder's analysis of an American Protestant: "There is no limit to the degree with which an American is imbued with the doctrine of progress. Place and environment are but décor to his journey. . . . He is what he is because his plans characterize him." This evaluation, made by the author twenty-five years after *The Bridge* was written, is still correct. Despite the general corruption, the economic inequities, the political ignorance, and the military tragedies to be found in certain Asiatic countries, the simple act of getting the population to vote—

whether or not it understands what it is doing—proves to many Americans that democracy is at work. (It was precisely this simplistic view of life that exasperated Charles Dickens a century before in *Martin Chuzzlewit.*) Few American writers, however severely they criticize their native land, do it as subtly, as gracefully, and as ironically as Wilder.

He has a little more fun with Brother Juniper in another capacity. Since the Franciscan looks upon it as his life's work to "justify the ways of God to man," he is forever keeping records, like a schoolteacher giving his students grades. He has, for instance, "a complete record of the Prayers for Rain and their results" (Americans are nothing if not pragmatists!). When the pestilence destroys a large number of peasants, he "secretly drew up a diagram of the characteristics of fifteen victims and fifteen survivors. . . . Each soul was rated upon a basis of ten as regards its goodness, its diligence in religious observance, and its importance to its family group." The only trouble is that after Brother Juniper finishes adding and subtracting and juggling his figures and statistics, he estimates "that the dead were five times more worth saving" than those who lived! He is badly shaken by the knowledge that "the discrepancy between faith and the facts is greater than is generally realized." George Brush is going to be shocked by the same discovery in *Heaven's My Destination.*

Yet while he has been busy collecting all the data about those who perished, Brother Juniper, a kind of eighteenth-century human computer, never really learns much about the five people he has studied. He gathers all the proper information, but what evades him is the central passion of their lives. At this point the narrator intrudes on the story and asks: "And I, who claim to know so much more, isn't it possible that even I have missed the very spring within the spring?" For the truth is, all human existence is a mystery, and no one can know everything about everyone. And even if one could, one could never understand the clockwork complications of the soul. The narrator concludes the first part:

> Some say that we shall never know and that to the gods we are like the flies that the boys kill on a summer day, and some say, on the contrary, that the very sparrows do not lose a feather that has not been brushed away by the finger of God.

THE VICTIMS

. . . The next three parts of *The Bridge* take up the lives of the people who were killed. The Marquesa de Montemayor, a middle-aged woman who has made an unhappy marriage, turns to her daughter, Doña Clara, as substitute for her lost emotional life and pours all her love out on the girl. Doña Clara, like James Blair in *The Cabala*, is a frigid young person with no love to give; further, she despises her mother's excessive demonstrations of affection. As quickly as she can she marries a Spanish grandee and returns with him to his home in Spain, leaving her mother in Peru. The Marquesa has only one outlet for her feelings: she turns to writing letters to her daughter as a means of binding them together, for literature "is the notation of the heart.". . .

Because of the Marquesa's loneliness the Abbess Madre Maria del Pilar sends a young girl, Pepita, to keep her company. Pepita loves the Abbess, suffers at leaving the convent, is unhappy with the Marquesa, and longs to return. She goes so far as to write a letter to the Abbess begging that she be allowed to come back—but she never sends the letter, for she knows that the best proof she can give the Abbess of her love is to do as she is bidden. In Pepita's love there is both self-discipline and self-sacrifice. The Marquesa, coming upon the letter "accidentally," understands for the first time how selfish her love for her daughter had been, how strong an element there was of a wish to dominate, to impress. . . .

The next section concerns the twin brothers Esteban and Manuel, who were abandoned as babies at the convent run by the Abbess. As they grow up they become more and more isolated from the world, more and more dependent on each other. They even have the knack of anticipating each other's wishes and wants without the need for speech. Between them there exists the bond that is lacking between the Marquesa and her daughter. But while the Marquesa is gradually moving in the direction of unselfish love, the love between the brothers, already too extreme, is tarnished by the intrusion of La Perichole, who arouses the passion of both brothers and for the first time awakens jealousy in their breasts.

Though Manuel and Esteban sincerely love each other, it is Manuel who feels more deeply. Recognizing that Esteban is suffering (La Perichole favors Manuel largely because he is a scribe who writes letters for her), Manuel gives her up.

Before long he has an accident, contracts a fever from an infected foot, and in his delirium cries out his love for La Perichole. Although Esteban has profited from his brother's sacrificial gesture of renunciation, he is plagued by guilt; when Manuel dies Esteban's collapse is so total that he refuses to be himself any longer and pretends that he is Manuel. . . . Esteban's moment of illumination comes when he realizes that self-destruction is not the answer. And at that moment of grace he crosses the bridge. . . .

The last section dealing with the other two victims is perhaps the least interesting, partly because of the characters, partly because Wilder has already made his point clearly enough and here simply repeats himself. Uncle Pio, alone in the world, has taken La Perichole into his profession and made a great actress out of her. She is a coarse, ignorant, vulgar woman; love, for her, is defined exclusively through sex. After a successful stage career and an interlude as the Viceroy's mistress, by whom she has three children, she leaves the stage. At the same time she suddenly discovers a craving for virtue and becomes more pious and proper than the most dedicated churchwoman. Finally she wearies of even this pose and embarks on a series of futile, furtive affairs.

Over the years Uncle Pio has learned something from his life and his amours: he never again "regarded any human being, from a prince to a servant, as a mechanical object." But not so Camilla, La Perichole. When he tells her of his devotion and wishes they could go away to some island where "the people would know [her] and love [her] for" herself, she laughs at him. "There is no such thing as that kind of love and that kind of island. It's in the theatre you find such things." La Perichole has never known real love. But she *has* known real art. And that, too, is a bridge.

Camilla and Uncle Pio drift apart until he discovers, again "accidentally," that she has been stricken with smallpox, and although she survives the disease, she loses all her beauty, of which she had been so vain. With its passing she knows that love will also die, for she had never been able to separate her beauty from the responses it evoked in her admirers: who could love her now that she was ugly and disfigured? And here the narrator interrupts to define the limitations of passion:

> Though it expends itself in generosity and thoughtfulness, though it give birth to visions and to great poetry, [it] remains

among the sharpest expressions of self-interest. Not until it has passed through a long servitude, through its own self-hatred, through mockery, through great doubts, can it take its place among the loyalties.

Uncle Pio, recognizing Camilla's complete spiritual shipwreck and anxious to salvage her little boy, Jaime, pleads with her to give the boy to him for a year. He loves Jaime, he wants to teach him, to raise him. And for the first time Camilla has an unselfish emotion: she consents to give the child up for his own good. Jaime will make a fresh start, Uncle Pio can renew himself in the boy, the future seems bright. As they draw near the bridge Uncle Pio tells Jaime that when they cross it "they would sit down and rest, but it turned out not to be necessary."

At the end of the novel Brother Juniper, having amassed all the necessary facts, which only baffle him since the key to the puzzle is missing, writes his book. The inferences he draws are confusing. Pepita was a good child, so was Jaime. Therefore the accident called the young to Heaven while they were still pure. On the other hand, Uncle Pio had led a dissolute life and the Marquesa was an avaricious drunkard. Therefore the accident punished the wicked. But how could the same accident perform two such different functions? In the midst of the friar's bafflement his book catches the eye of certain judges, who decide poor Brother Juniper is guilty of heresy because he has presumed to explain God's plan. As he sits in his cell awaiting punishment in the flames, he ponders over the riddle, anxious to find some meaning in his own demise, which would not be unwelcome if it brought some illumination. But he never finds the answer he is seeking; he simply calls upon St. Francis (feeling too inferior to invoke God at the moment of death), and leans upon a flame and dies, smiling.

FINDING THE MEANING

The funeral of the victims on the bridge brings together all those who were left behind. The Marquesa's daughter visits the Abbess, showing her mother's last letter and her transformation. La Perichole visits the Abbess and tells her of Esteban, Pepita, Uncle Pio, and Jaime. Before their deaths the five characters had, in Catholic terms, entered a state of grace, and by their deaths they have transformed those whom they loved. It does not matter that in a little while no one will remember them. For the Abbess knows:

> . . . soon we shall die and all memory of those five will have
> left the earth, and we ourselves shall be loved for a while and
> forgotten. But the love will have been enough; all those
> impulses of love return to the love that made them. Even
> memory is not necessary for love. There is a land of the liv-
> ing and a land of the dead and the bridge is love, the only sur-
> vival, the only meaning.

Every type of love is scrutinized in this novel: primitive
sexual love, exaggerated fraternal love, one-sided mother
love. All are, in one way or another, impure. But all pass
through a kind of filter that drains off the dross, and what is
left is the Christian *agape*—people loving each other in the
same way God loves them. . . .

So, although Brother Juniper did not prove to his satisfaction that there was any design in the fall of the bridge, or in
the deaths of the five who were present, those who read the
book know that there was a meaning in these events, after
all. By laying the story before us, the narrator enables us to
see further than Brother Juniper, even as God, the Narrator,
can see beyond us. It is safe to say that those with religious
beliefs feel buttressed by *The Bridge of San Luis Rey;* those
without them remain politely skeptical. For this is the final
lesson of the novel: that faith has nothing to do with reason.
If Brother Juniper had accepted instead of trying to prove, he
would never have needed to write his book. And so need
never have died.

QUESTIONING NIHILISM

It makes small sense, then, to quarrel with the book's theology, as some critics have done, a few arguing that every incident tries so hard to pile up proof of the "intention" that the
book collapses, like the bridge, under such an artificial
weight of evidence. . . . On its own terms *The Bridge* works;
its very timelessness, its suspension in space, may in fact
allow it to endure longer than other works of a different cast
published during the same period—for example, the once-
relevant, newspaperlike novels of John Dos Passos. It is
almost as though Wilder had examined the exiles inhabiting
the universe of Ernest Hemingway's *The Sun Also Rises,* the
idle and the sybaritic who waft through F. Scott Fitzgerald's
The Great Gatsby, the poor and the outcast who populate
Sidney Kingsley's *Dead End,* and said, "Yes, there is death;
yes, there is boredom; yes, there is poverty and despair. But
are you quite sure there is nothing else?" While most

American writers of the time were busy showing the reading public an earth cut off from the light by a moral or economic eclipse, Wilder was gently reminding us that the sun was still there and that the darkness would have to pass for the simple reason that Nature had so ordained it. *The Bridge of San Luis Rey* remains a tribute to its author's particular vision, his uncompromising integrity as an artist, and—a peculiarly American virtue—his rugged individualism.

Wilder's Intent in *The Bridge of San Luis Rey*

Malcolm Goldstein

Malcolm Goldstein has written on drama and theater subjects ranging from Restoration drama to George S. Kaufman; he is also the author of *The Political Stage: American Drama and Theater of the Great Depression*. In this excerpt from his book *The Art of Thornton Wilder*, Goldstein discusses *The Bridge of San Luis Rey*, including the reasons Wilder set it in eighteenth-century Peru. He finds that *The Bridge* offers a philosophy that focuses on the individual—one that he says has been missed by those readers and critics who see in it a presentation of Christian themes.

The history of *The Bridge of San Luis Rey* . . . has included two Hollywood productions, a television adaptation, and continuous availability in a variety of hardcover and softbound printings, in addition to the Pulitzer Prize. From the outset, it has been a popular favorite.

Turning away from the modern world for the time being, Wilder set his new novel in eighteenth-century Peru. The setting is so distant from the areas explored by most of the established writers of the 1920's that Wilder's reasons for choosing it have frequently come under question. This was, after all, the decade when Willa Cather's tough-minded novels of the prairies and the Southwest were achieving the status of minor classics as soon as published, when Sinclair Lewis, for all his roughness of style, reached the best-seller lists with each novel of the Midwest, and when even the expatriates Ernest Hemingway and Gertrude Stein wrote with a patently deep attachment to their homeland. In attempting to account for Wilder's neglect of America in his fiction, Malcolm Cowley has suggested that, unlike his famous contemporaries, he has never lived long enough in any one region to put down roots in American soil.[1] He had spent his formative years not in one or (like Willa Cather) two places, but in Wisconsin, California, China, and California again, and having so many homes, he has none so distinctly his that it could serve as a base upon which to erect a fictional image of his country. . . .

MAKING USE OF HIS LEARNING

Of nearly equal consequence in the making of *The Bridge* was the range and continuity of Wilder's learning. As both an instinctive and academic scholar, he was inevitably persuaded by his researches to give them shape in his fiction. His recent study in Romance languages at Princeton makes itself apparent in *The Bridge,* through allusions to Spanish literature of the Golden Age, through his fashioning of one character, the Marquesa de Montemayor, upon the personality and literary pursuits of Mme. de Sévigné, and through the borrowing of another, Camilla Perichole, from Prosper Mérimée's *La Carosse du Saint Sacré,* which also provides the setting. The desire is always present in the scholar to make extensive use of his learning. With Wilder it manifested itself in fiction and drama, not, as with most academic men, in biographical, philological, or critical essays, though the initial impulse is the same for all. Considering this root quality in the scholarly personality, it is reasonable to say that the civilizations which Wilder had studied were as vivid to him as the life of his own time and place. That he had not traveled to Peru was of no consequence to him. Three decades later he remarked to an interviewer from the *Paris Review* that "the journey of the imagination to a remote place is child's play compared to a journey into another time. I've often been in New York, but it's just as preposterous to write about the New York of 1812 as to write about the Incas."[2]

Another influence, apparent in *The Cabala* also, was the humanistic criticism of More and Babbitt.[3] It manifests itself in two aspects of Wilder's art: the absence of violence and squalor and the acceptance of Christian values. In the first and second episodes of *The Cabala* Wilder describes the exotic col-

---

1. Malcolm Cowley, introduction, *A Thornton Wilder Trio* (New York: Criterion Books, 1956), p. 4. 2. Richard H. Goldstone, "Thornton Wilder," in *Writers at Work: The Paris Review Interviews,* ed. Malcolm Cowley (New York: Viking Press, 1958), pp. 104–105. 3. Paul Elmer More (1864–1937), U.S. essayist and critic, and Irving Babbitt (1865–1933), U.S. educator and critic, were the founders of the modern humanistic movement, which holds that human interests, values, and dignity are paramount and rejects the importance of a belief in God.

oration given to life by troubled belief; although he is sometimes scornful of or impatient with the wrong-headed characters of that novel, his tone is for the most part only mildly
ironic. He treats this subject again in *The Bridge*, but in a quite
different mode. We should note that the setting is a place
where the relationship of God to man made itself felt in all the
details of life, as it does not in twentieth-century America.

Finding the Spring Within the Spring

Structurally as well as thematically, *The Bridge of San Luis Rey*
resembles *The Cabala*. Wilder again employs a sketchy fram-
ing story to bring unity to three tales which are only partially
related in content. There are, however, certain differences in
the use of this device in the second novel, but not such as work
to Wilder's advantage. In the frame of *The Bridge*, the function
of Samuele goes to a young, earnest Franciscan friar, Brother
Juniper, who resembles Samuele in his presumptuousness,
but does not narrate the events and does not take part in them.
His presence is little more than an excuse for the three
episodes, and that little serves only to establish his own interpretation of them, which eventually Wilder overthrows in
favor of a superior interpretation. When Brother Juniper, on a
day in 1714, sees an old slat-and-vine bridge near Lima break
and send five travelers to death in the gorge below, he begins
a search through the history of their lives for pieces of evidence that God purposely let them die, for he is certain that the
event is no accident. The five are an old man, a middle-aged
woman, a young man, an adolescent girl, and a little boy.
Unlike the characters of *The Cabala*, they have not all played
important roles in one another's lives, and none has known
the young man who now takes a surpassing interest in them.
Compared to Samuele's old-maidish fussing over the
Cabalists, which in itself contributes abundantly to the theme
of the narrative, Brother Juniper's presence is an ungainly
expository contrivance, and his by-the-book religiosity, weigh-
ing so much good in each victim of the fall against so much
evil, is too obviously unavailing in the search for the meaning
of the disaster.

"Yet for all his diligence," the omniscient author says,
"Brother Juniper never knew the central passion of Doña
Maria's life; nor of Uncle Pio's, not even of Esteban's. And I,
who claim to know so much more, isn't it possible that even I
have missed the very spring within the spring?" Thus taking

the reader into his confidence with the suggestion that any system for measuring the quality of a life is certain to fail, Wilder begins the three short episodes which lead the five travelers up to the fatal moment. He himself does not give a direct interpretation of the event, but leaves it to the reader to discover what common concerns of all five have caused them to walk simultaneously over the bridge to death. In the last pages of the novel the alert reader's findings are given voice by Madre Maria del Pilar, Abbess of the Convent of Santa Maria de las Rosas, the one character who has knowledge of the entire group of victims:

> "Even now," she thought, "almost no one remembers Esteban and Pepita, but myself. Camila alone remembers her Uncle Pio and her son; this woman, her mother. But soon we shall die and all memory of those five will have left the earth, and we our-selves shall be loved for a while and forgotten. But the love will have been enough; all those impulses of love return to the love that made them. Even memory is not necessary for love. There is a land of the living and a land of the dead and the bridge is love, the only survival, the only meaning."

By this time the "spring within the spring" of each life has come to light, and for each it is the same: the desire for love. The episodes demonstrate that the fall of the bridge is actual-ly a spring *into* love; on this point the deliberations of Brother Juniper, as well as the brief first-person comments of the author, are dust thrown into the reader's eyes, as though pur-posely to make difficult the analysis of a novel which is by no means complex. . . .

In review, the victims of the bridge are these: an old woman whose daughter spurns her affection, an adolescent girl who lives only for the affection of an older woman, a young man whose sole object of love is dead, an old man whose sole object of love has rejected him, and a child whose mother is too self-involved to give him the affection he requires. For one reason or another, each stands apart from human society: two because they are old and unkempt; two because they are orphans; and the fifth because he is chronically ill. And with the exception of Don Jaime, each has added to the barrier between himself and society by failing to respond to any activ-ity which does not involve his beloved. Pepita is at only slight-ly greater odds with the rest of humanity than Don Jaime, but even she must think constantly of the one person she loves in order to sustain herself, and it is not until she begins to recog-nize the selfishness inherent in her distress in the Marquesa's household that she is allowed to escape through death. Perhaps it is a flaw in the novel that Don Jaime's life so poorly fits the pattern set by the other characters; yet he resembles them in part by agreeing to leave his mother, the only person whom he adores, and to go down to Lima with Uncle Pio. But, for that matter, Wilder flatly asserts that it is difficult, if not impossible, to find patterns in existence, and Brother Juniper is burned as a heretic for trying to do so.

WHAT MOST READERS—AND CRITICS—MISS

Although *The Bridge of San Luis Rey* is imperfect, its faults are not ruinous. Whatever they may be, they are not caused by such deficiencies in taste and wisdom as are evident in most American religious fiction—the novels of Lloyd C. Douglas provide suitable examples for comparison. *The Bridge* is not sentimental; it offers no promises of earthly rewards and no overestimation of the worth of the characters. Nor does it speak out against active participation in this life in favor of patient waiting for the life to come. Yet, noting that many persons have misunderstood his intention, Wilder has himself remarked: "only one reader in a thousand notices that I have asserted a denial of the survival of identity after death."[4] While it is true, as this comment suggests, that many find the book "inspirational" and read it precisely as they read Bishop Fulton J. Sheen's *Peace of Soul* or Rabbi Joshua Loth Liebmann's *Peace of Mind*, it is difficult to understand how they could be misled. For, far from recommending a narcotic contemplation of the afterlife, Wilder speaks out for the vigorous pursuit of purely human relationships. If the five characters are tragic, they are so not because they die suddenly, or simply because they die, but because they have not truly lived, and at no point are we led to think that they will win the reward of an eventual reunion in heaven with the recipients of the love that for so many years enchained them. Threading through the narrative is the career of the Abbess, whose closeness to the life of Lima and attentiveness to everyday events are a reminder of the indifference of the others to such matters in their pursuit of a single goal. None of the victims escapes the measurement of his personality against that of this very vital woman. The consecration of her life to a program of work for the good of all humanity, involving her in the sacri-

---

4. Wilder to Paul Friedman, undated letter, in Friedman, "The Bridge: A Study in Symbolism," *Psychoanalytic Quarterly*, XXI (Jan. 1952), 72.

fice of Pepita, Manuel, and Esteban, puts to shame the selfishness of the others as it is reflected in their indulgence in the anguish of love. In *The Bridge*, as in *The Cabala* and the major works which followed, Wilder insists that the life that is a rush of unanalyzed activity is as nothing when compared to the life in which the participant allows himself to become fully aware of the meaning of each experience.

Unhappily, Wilder's latter-day critics have served him no better than his most naive readers. Impatient with the slow-moving, aphoristic style and the historical setting, they have looked back on *The Bridge* as a kind of sport among the popular novels of the 1920's and mention it as such if they mention it at all. It is true that this work contrasts bleakly with the naturalistic novels which now seem to be the sum of the literature of the decade, but to admit that fact is not to deny its quality. However much it may differ in technique from the fiction of, say, Hemingway, Fitzgerald, or John Dos Passos, it does not display a soft attitude toward the human condition. At the time of its publication it offered a considerable change in tone from the fast-paced novels of the age, and obviously a welcome change in view of the sales record, but it did not offer easy lessons in contentment.

CHAPTER 4

Pulitzer #2:
Our Town

Our Town's Big and Little Wheels

Winfield Townley Scott

As *Our Town* begins, writes Winfield Townley Scott, the playwright sets in motion the little wheel of everyday activities in Grover's Corners. The town's inhabitants are interesting and touching because of—rather than in spite of—their symbolic nature. The narrator, who is not bound by time, intersperses his descriptions of the ordinary activities of the scene onstage with mentions of future events, so the audience becomes aware of the turning of the big wheel—time itself, carrying the weight of births, marriages, deaths. At first, Scott points out, only the narrator and the audience are privy to this split view. But when Emily returns from the dead for just one day—"the least important day" in her life—every detail of that day stands out in poignant recognition of the need to live life fully as it happens. Winfield Townley Scott, a reviewer and poet, was literary editor of the *Providence (R.I.) Journal.*

Perhaps the germination of *Our Town* is in the legend Chrysis tells her young men in *The Woman of Andros,* that slender novel of the dying Grecian spirit which Wilder published eight years before his play. Chrysis tells of a dead hero for whom Zeus interceded with the King of the Dead and to whom it was permitted "to live over again that day in all the twenty-two thousand days of his lifetime that had been least eventful; but that it must be with a mind divided into two persons,—the participant and the onlooker: the participant who does the deeds and says the words of so many years before, and the onlooker who foresees the end. So the hero returned to the sunlight and to a certain day in his fifteenth year."

From "*Our Town* and the Golden Veil," by Winfield Townley Scott, *Virginia Quarterly Review*, Winter 1953. Reprinted with permission.

"'My friends,' continued Chrysis, turning her eyes slowly from face to face, 'as he awoke in his boyhood's room, pain filled his heart,—not only because it had started beating again, but because he saw the walls of his home and knew that in a moment he would see his parents who lay long since in the earth of that country. He descended into the courtyard. His mother lifted her eyes from the loom and greeted him and went on with her work. His father passed through the court unseeing, for on that day his mind had been full of care. Suddenly the hero saw that the living too are dead and that we can only be said to be alive in those moments when our hearts are conscious of our treasure; for our hearts are not strong enough to love every moment. And not an hour had gone by before the hero *who was both watching life and living it* called on Zeus to release him from so terrible a dream. The gods heard him, but before he left he fell upon the ground and kissed the soil of the world that is too dear to be realized.'"

At *Our Town* the audience is the resurrected hero.

Birth; marriage; death: these are the respective keynotes of the three acts as they are of most lives. In Act I, birth is used only as a momentary tone and for its symbolic sake: Dr. Gibbs is on his way home at dawn from delivering, "easy as kittens," Mrs. Goruslawski's twins. Wilder extends the symbol of birth to compose an innocent picture of ordinary daily life, the seemingly unimportant trivia of the middleclass at school, at its jobs, at church, and in its homes in a New England small town. Here are a group of people and their relationships. He gives us, in Robert Hillyer's phrase, the "pattern of a day." It is not, on its obvious level, impinged upon by the great—and ordinary—ceremonies which mark Acts II and III.

It is a specific day. The Stage Manager sets it as he will continue to arrange and comment upon everything to follow. It is May 7, 1901. Nearly dawn. We are given the idea of what size and sort of town this is—"Nice town, y' know what I mean?"—and its rhythms begin. The 5:45 to Boston whistles through. Joe Crowell, Jr., starts his rounds delivering Editor Webb's newspaper. Howie Newsome's milk wagon appears— Mrs. Gibbs thinks Howie is a bit late today, which he is: "Somep'n went wrong with the separator." Both Mrs. Webb and Mrs. Gibbs are soon calling upstairs to their young- sters—Wally and Emily Webb, and George and Rebecca

Gibbs—to get a move on, hurry to breakfast and to school: as, one is sure, Mrs. Webb and Mrs. Gibbs holler up every schoolday in the year. And Dr. Gibbs, as I say, is just coming in from delivering Mrs. Goruslawski's twins. With his appearance on stage the scheme of *Our Town* quietly clicks into action. The scheme is hinted, even revealed, a moment or so before; now it really begins.

THE LITTLE WHEEL

As *Our Town* literally begins, Wilder sets in motion the little wheel of daily doings. This is the only wheel there is in most plays and fictions; it turns upon the events presented. So here, it spins with normal activities, the comings and goings and the conversations, weaving a special era and place and a particular people (though by the way I think Mrs. Gibbs and Mrs. Webb should not be stringing beans in early May in New Hampshire); and on through a gentle afternoon to the great moonlighted night of that May 7 and the ladies strolling chattering home from choir practice

This is the realism of the play and, superficially at least, it is very good. That is, these folk may not be deeply imagined but they are typically imagined; it is as types of Americana that they and their Grover's Corners interest us and touch us. They and the town are unremarkable: we are told so and we see that it is so; and this of course is the point. The youngsters with their twenty-five cents spending-money and love of strawberry phosphates and their schoolday affairs, the fathers absorbed in jobs and bringing up these young, the wives similarly absorbed though perhaps a little wistfully aware of larger worlds and startled at just this era that an old highboy might fetch $350 as an antique; yes, we are convinced that this must have been the way it was, and in most essentials still is fifty years later, in that kind of American town. For what the little wheel does in carrying these doings of realism is to give one a sense of changelessness from day to day, year to year: mothers and fathers waken early, they rouse children to breakfast and school, a Joe Crowell, Jr., always comes along with the newspaper and Howie Newsome with the milk; there is talk of weather which does change season to season but the changes are regular and assured. Far later in the play the Stage Manager remarks something we have known from the first, and known with an intimate feeling, and are not surprised as he said we would be—"on the whole, things don't change much at Grover's Corners."

Thus this little wheel gives us a sense of timeliness and also, oddly, of timelessness. We are transported back to May 7, 1901. At the same time we sense a certain universality about it; or we sense its *being* as a seemingly permanent thing. And this achievement is the one for which so much writing strives. Nevertheless, we are quickly aware of another dimension which begins to operate when Dr. Gibbs comes on.

We have learned a little earlier that though this is May 7, 1901, in Grover's Corners, New Hampshire, and though the townsman who appears to us as the Stage Manager is there presenting us with this scene and time, he is also existing in our time. He describes stores, streets, schools, churches in the present tense (and this forwards the feeling of changelessness within change as the newly discovered context is revealed), but he suddenly says, "First automobile's going to come along in about five years." And presently: "There's Doc Gibbs comin' down Main Street now. . . . Doc Gibbs died in 1930. The new hospital's named after him. Mrs. Gibbs died first—long time ago in fact. She went out to visit her daughter, Rebecca, who married an insurance man in Canton, Ohio, and died there—pneumonia . . ." and so on. "In our town we like to know the facts about everybody," he sums up matter of factly; and then: "That's Doc Gibbs." And Dr. Gibbs gets into a little gab with Joe Crowell, Jr., just as Mrs. Gibbs is seen entering her kitchen to start breakfast.

THE BIG WHEEL

The whole tone of *Our Town* is understatement. The colloquial run of the talk, its occasional dry wit, the unheroic folk, all contribute to this tone. So does the important admission that this *is* a play: we are not bid to suspend our disbelief in the usual way; and so does the bareboard, undecorated presentation. All is simple, modest, easy, plain. And so, in tone, the Stage Manager's revelation is utterly casual. But with it Wilder sets in counter-motion to the little wheel a big wheel; and as the little one spins the little doings, the big one begins slowly—slowly—for it is time itself, weighted with birth and marriage and death, with aging and with change. This is the great thing that *Our Town* accomplishes; simultaneously we are made aware of what is momentary and what is eternal.

We are involved by the Stage Manager in these presented actions and yet like him we are also apart; we are doubly spectators, having a double vision. We are not asked, as in the presentation of some philosophical concept, to perceive an abstract intellectualism. This is a play—this is art. So we are involved sensually and emotionally. Out of shirt-sleeved methods that would seem to defy all magic, and because of them not in spite of them, Wilder's play soon throttles us with its pathos; convinces and moves us so that we cannot imagine its being done in any other way; assumes a radiant beauty. And indeed we are not taken out of ourselves, we are driven deeper into ourselves. This, we say, is life: apparently monotonous, interminable, safe; really all mutable, brief, and in danger. "My," sighs the dead Mrs. Soames in Act III, "wasn't life awful—and wonderful." For what Wilder's art has reminded us is that beauty is recognizable because of change and life is meaningful because of death.

Later in Act I the Stage Manager deliberately and directly accounts for several future happenings. And again he sums up: "So, friends, this was the way we were in our growing up and in our marrying and in our doctoring and in our living and in our dying." This is the simplest way—and Thornton Wilder can be artfully simple—of saying what *Our Town* is about. It suggests why he chose a spare, documentary style as appropriate to his purpose. But the poetry, so to speak, comes from the juxtaposition of the points of view, human and superhuman, which combine, of course, to a fourth dimension. . . .

LACONIC YANKEE WIT

The wit is Yankee laconic; sometimes so wry you may ask if it is wit. Noting that lights are on in the distant farmhouses while most of Grover's Corners itself is still dark at six o'clock in the morning, the Stage Manager says, "But town people sleep late." It is funny—but is it funny to the Stage Manager? We have no way of knowing that the Stage Manager does not feel that people who don't get up till six-thirty or seven are late sleepers. This is a part of the charm.

The charm does not evade the big and the ephemeral troubles of life, the tears of youth and of age, and the terminal fact of death. As *Our Town* develops, it is more and more incandescent with the charges of change and of ending. There is not in it any of the ugliness present in the small town books I have likened it to: the violence and murder in *Tom Sawyer*, the meannesses and frustrations in *Spoon River Anthology* and *Winesburg, Ohio*. Yet these books also glow with a nostalgic beauty. True, the drunken, disappointed organist would be at home either in Masters' Spoon River or in Robinson's Tilbury Town; and in Act II, at the time of George's wedding, there is the bawdiness of the baseball players which, significantly, the Stage Manager quickly hushes. Brief touches: not much. Nevertheless, I would defend *Our Town* against the instant, obvious question whether Wilder in excluding harsher facts indigenous to life has written a sentimental play, by insisting Wilder would have warped the shape of his plan by such introductions. He was out not to compose a complete small-town history nor, on the other hand, to expose a seamy-sided one; his evident purpose was to dramatize the common essentials of the lives of average people. There are other colors, no doubt more passionate, but they would have deranged this simple purpose which, as I see it, is valid and has been well-served.

I do not know whether a great deal has been written about this play; I happen to have seen only a retrospective note by John Mason Brown. That is chiefly a paean of praise for the durable loveliness of *Our Town*, but Mr. Brown feels that Act III—the death act—loses the universality of the other two by being too colloquial and by serving forth "small ideas." I think this critic, and he is a fine critic, has hit to one side of a target which is there. It is not that Act III has a small idea; it has a very large one—the theory of death which the Stage Manager announces:

"You know as well as I do," he says, "that the dead don't stay interested in us living people for very long. Gradually . . ." and so on: readying us for the indifferent attitude of the dead and for the newly dead Emily's bewildered approach to it. This I would say is neither small nor too colloquial but too easy; it is too major a premise in the play to be tossed in casually. It cannot in itself carry conviction. The colloquialism of Act III, meanwhile, is proper to the tone of all that has gone before. We accept it and, presently, the conception of the dead because of the emotional power of the play's final passages. They throb with an accumulative and transcending strength.

The crisscross of feelings over the wedding in Act II starts the beat of an emotional pulse: the fear and love of the parents, the fear and desire of Emily and George, shudder in terror and wonder. Here is the new adult experience, central to most lives: marriage. It has its humor, for it is common; its pathos, for it is doomed. "No love story," Ernest Hemingway has remarked, "has a happy ending." By a leap of nine years we are plunged directly in Act III to the remaining enormous fact, death: Emily's death, while still young, in her second childbearing; Emily's death a matter of moments, so it seems, after her wedding.

"THINGS DON'T CHANGE MUCH"

It is twelve years since the literal time of Act I; it is the summer of 1913, and now the play vibrates with its full magic. Once again the Stage Manager sets the scene. He is in the Grover's Corners cemetery, but he lets us know that horses are rarer in the town, Fords frequenter, the youngsters avid for the movies. "Everybody locks their doors now at night. . . . But you'd be surprised though—on the whole, things don't change much at Grover's Corners." We now have the sense of knowing this town and its people a long while. "Here's your friend, Mrs. Gibbs," the Stage Manager says, pacing among the dead on the hill. "Here is Mr. Stimson, organist at the Congregational Church. And over there's Mrs. Soames who enjoyed the wedding so—you remember? . . . And Editor Webb's boy, Wallace . . ." and so on.

Now the "eternal" theme, counterpointed still to the little wheel, is carried by the dead; though with rural chatter. They talk of the weather, of George's barn on his uncle's farm; we discover from mention of Mrs. Gibbs' "legacy" of $350 to George and Emily that she must have sold that highboy she talked about in 1901 and that after all she did not persuade the doctor to travel on the money to Paris, France. Yes, we know them intimately, these emotionless dead and the grieving living townspeople who soon will come bearing young Emily to her grave.

Emily appears, to take her place with the dead. Already she is distant from the mourners, but her discovery that she can "go back" to past time seduces her despite the warnings of the older dead. The ubiquitous Stage Manager, too, can talk with Emily, and what he says to her introduces the summation scene with the keynote of the entire play: "You not only live it," he says, "but you watch yourself living it." Now

Emily, in the yet more poignant way of self-involvement, will achieve that double vision we have had all along; and now we shall be burdened also with her self-involvement.

"And as you watch it," the Stage Manager goes on, "you will see the thing that they—down there—never know. You see the future. You know what's going to happen afterwards."

Then perfectly in key comes Mrs. Gibbs' advice to Emily: "At least, choose an unimportant day. Choose the least important day in your life. It will be important enough." There sound the central chords of the play: the common day and the light of the future.

Unbearable Tension

Emily chooses her twelfth birthday and the magic begins to mount to almost unbearable tension. Now the Stage Manager repeats his enrichened gesture as he announces that it is February 11, 1899, and once again, as we saw him summon it in the same casual way so many years before, the town of Grover's Corners stirs, awakens; a winter morning—Constable Warren, Howie Newsome, Joe Crowell, Jr., making their appearances along Main Street, Mrs. Webb firing the kitchen stove and calling Wally and Emily to breakfast. The little daily rhythms recur, now more touching for the big wheel has become vaster. Now *we* are taken back with Emily's double-awareness accenting our own. Though the then-living are unaware as always, now the golden veil [of nostalgia] shines everywhere, even all around us ourselves. It is a terrific triumph of dramatic method.

"Oh, that's the town I knew as a little girl. And, look, there is the old white fence that used to be around our house. Oh, I'd forgotten that! . . . I can't look at everything hard enough," Emily says. "There's Mr. Morgan's drugstore. And there's the High School, forever and ever, and ever." For her birthday young George Webb has left a postcard album on the doorstep: Emily had forgotten that.

The living cannot hear the dead Emily of fourteen years later, her whole lifetime later. Yet she cries out in the passion, which the play itself performs, to realize life while it is lived: "But, just for a moment now we're all together. Mama, just for a moment we're happy. Let's look at one another." And when offstage her father's voice is heard a second time calling, "Where's my girl? Where's my birthday girl?" Emily breaks. She flees back through the future, back to the patient and disinterested dead: "Oh," she says of life, "it goes so fast. We don't have time to look at one another."

Here if the play is to get its proper and merited response there is nothing further to say of it: one simply weeps.

It is thus, finally, that Emily can say farewell to the world— that is, to Grover's Corners. Night, now; the night after Emily's burial. The big wheel of the mutable universe turns almost alone. The Stage Manager notices starlight and its "millions of years," but time ticks eleven o'clock on his watch and the town, though there, is mostly asleep, as he dismisses us for "a good rest, too."

The aptest thing ever said about *Tom Sawyer* was said by the author himself and applies as nicely to *Our Town*. Mark Twain said his book was "a hymn."

A Contemporary Review

Mary McCarthy

Novelist Mary McCarthy (*The Company She Keeps, A Charmed Life*) was the radical *Partisan Review*'s theater critic–a job that was hers at first, she says, "because I had been married to an actor." In her review of *Our Town*, McCarthy says the play is innovative, intense, and poignant.

Mr. Thornton Wilder's play, . . . *Our Town*, like *Ah, Wilderness,* is an exercise in memory, but it differs from the O'Neill work in that it is not a play in the accepted sense of the term. It is essentially lyric, not dramatic. The tragic velocity of life, the elusive nature of experience, which can never be stopped or even truly felt at any given point, are the themes of the play—themes familiar enough in lyric poetry, but never met, except incidentally, in drama. Mr. Wilder, in attempting to give these themes theatrical form, was obliged, paradoxically, to abandon almost all the conventions of the theatre.

In the first place, he has dismissed scenery and props as irrelevant to, and, indeed, incongruous with his purpose. In the second place, he has invented the character of the stage manager, an affable, homespun conjuror who holds the power of life and death over the other characters, a local citizen who is in the town and outside of it at the same time. In the third place, he has taken what is accessory to the ordinary play, that is, exposition, and made it the main substance of his. The greater part of the first two acts is devoted to the imparting of information, to situating the town in time, space, politics, sociology, economics, and geology. But where in the conventional play, such pieces of information are insinuated into the plot or sugared over with stage business and repartee, in Mr. Wilder's play they are communicated directly; they take the place of plot, stage business, and

From *Sights and Spectacles, 1937–1956,* by Mary McCarthy (New York: Farrar, Straus & Cudahy, 1956). Reprinted by permission of the Mary McCarthy Literary Trust. Subheadings in this reprint have been added by Greenhaven editors.

repartee. Mr. Craven himself tells the biographies of the townspeople; he calls in an expert from the state college to give a scientific picture of the town, and the editor of the local newspaper to describe its social conditions. The action which is intermittently progressing on the stage merely illustrates Mr. Craven's talk.

RAISING THE DEAD

Mr. Wilder's fourth innovation is the most striking. In order to dramatize his feelings about life he has literally raised the dead. At the opening of the third act a group of people are discovered sitting in rows on one side of the stage; some of the faces are familiar, some are new. They are speaking quite naturally and calmly, and it is not until one has listened to them for some minutes that one realizes that this is the cemetery and these are the dead. A young woman whom we have seen grow up and marry the boy next door has died in childbirth; a small shabby funeral procession is bringing her to join her relatives and neighbors. Only when she is actually buried does the play proper begin. She has not yet reached the serenity of the long dead, and she yearns to return to the world. With the permission of the stage manager and against the advice of the dead, she goes back—to a birthday of her childhood. Hardly a fraction of that day has passed, however, before she retreats gratefully to the cemetery, for she has perceived that the tragedy of life lies in the fragmentary and imperfect awareness of the living.

Mr. Wilder's play is, in a sense, a refutation of its own thesis. *Our Town* is purely and simply an act of awareness, a demonstration of the fact that in a work of art, at least, experience *can* be arrested, imprisoned, and preserved. The perspective of death, which Mr. Wilder has chosen, gives an extra poignancy and intensity to the small-town life whose essence he is trying so urgently to communicate. The little boy delivering papers, for example, becomes more touching, more meaningful and important, when Mr. Craven announces casually that he is going to be killed in the War. The boy's morning round, for the spectator, is transfigured into an absorbing ritual; the unconsciousness of the character has heightened the consciousness of the audience. The perspective is, to be sure, hazardous: it invites bathos and sententiousness. Yet Mr. Wilder has used it honorably. He forbids the spectator to dote on that town of the past. He is

IT TOOK COURAGE TO ADMIT SHE LIKED IT

When Mary McCarthy wrote this review of Our Town, *she was, in her own words, "a young, earnest, pedantic, pontificating critic"—yet she was also unsure about her own feelings. She was taken aback by the fact that she enjoyed Wilder's highly successful play, as she explains here.*

It is the voice of a period, as well as that of a person. The period was 1937. The place was downtown, in the old Bible House on Astor Place, where *Partisan Review,* a radical literary magazine, had just opened its offices, after a break with the Communist Party over the Moscow Trials. The young men who were editing the new magazine, except one (the backer) were Marxists. I was not one, but I took my line, as well as I could, from them. We automatically suspected any commercial success, any *succès d'estime;* this, I fear, was my guiding critical principle. I remember how uneasy I felt when I decided that I *liked* Thornton Wilder's *Our Town.* Could this mean that there was something the matter with me? Was I starting to sell out? Such haunting fears, like the fear of impotence in men, were common in the avant-garde in those days. The safest position was to remain always on the attack.

Mary McCarthy, *Sights and Spectacles, 1937–1956.* New York: Farrar, Straus and Cudahy, 1956.

concerned only with saying: this is how it was, though then we did not know it. Once in a while, of course, his memory fails him, for young love was never so baldly and tritely gauche as his scene in the soda fountain suggests. This is, however, a deficiency of imagination, not an error of taste; and except in the third act, where the dead give some rather imprecise and inapposite definitions of the nature of the afterlife, the play keeps its balance beautifully. In this feat of equilibrium Mr. Wilder has had the complete cooperation of Mr. Craven, the serene, inexorable matter-of-factness of whose performance acts as a discipline upon the audience. Mr. Craven makes one quite definitely homesick, but pulls one up sharp if one begins to blubber about it.

CHAPTER 5

Pulitzer #3:
The Skin of Our Teeth

Comparing *Finnegans Wake* with *The Skin of Our Teeth*

Joseph Campbell and Henry Morton Robinson

Joseph Campbell and Henry Morton Robinson had been working on a "key" to James Joyce's *Finnegans Wake* for three years when *The Skin of Our Teeth* opened in New York. They found many similarities in the two works, some of which they spelled out in articles in the December 19, 1942, and February 13, 1943, issues of *Saturday Review of Literature*. They stopped short of accusing Wilder of plagiarism, and indeed seemed unsure how to characterize their discovery at first, but the articles raised a storm of controversy that resulted in a flurry of essays and letters in several magazines. Wilder, like Campbell and Robinson, had been studying and lecturing on parts of *Finnegans Wake* for some time (he had delivered an hour-and-a-half lecture on seven pages of the book), but it is safe to say that few of those who joined the fray on either side had read more than a few sentences of that difficult volume. Campbell and Robinson's *Skeleton Key to Finnegans Wake* was published in 1961. Robinson also wrote a novel, *The Great Snow*, and *Fantastic Interim*, a look at recent American history. Campbell has written and edited many books on myth, religion, and philosophy, including *The Hero with a Thousand Faces* and *The Masks of God*.

While thousands cheer, no one has yet pointed out that Mr. Thornton Wilder's exciting play, *The Skin of Our Teeth*, is not an entirely original creation, but an Americanized re-creation, thinly disguised, of James Joyce's *Finnegans Wake*. Mr. Wilder himself goes out of his way to wink at the knowing one or two in the audience, by quoting from and actually naming some of his characters after the main figures of Joyce's masterpiece. Important plot elements, characters, devices of presentation, as well as major themes and many of the speeches, are directly and frankly imitated, with but the flimsiest veneer to lend an American touch to the original features.

The Skin of Our Teeth takes its circular form from *Finnegans Wake*, closing and opening with the cycle-renewing river-running thought-stream of the chief female character. The main divisions of the play are closed by periodic catastrophes (ice-age, deluge, war), devices which are borrowed from the cosmic dissolutions of *Finnegans Wake*. Furthermore, Mr. Antrobus, Thornton Wilder's hero, is strangely reminiscent of Joyce's protagonist, H.C. Earwicker, "that homogenius man," who has endured throughout all the ages of the world, though periodically overwhelmed by floods, wars, and other catastrophes. The activities, talents, and troubles of the two characters have significant resemblances. In both works they are Adam, All-Father of the world. They are tireless inventors and land-conquerors; both are constantly sending communiques back home; both run for election, broadcast to the world, and are seen in television. Moreover, their characters have been impugned. In each case the hero repudiates the charges against him, but the secret guilt which each seeks to hide is constantly betrayed by slips of the tongue. To add to the long list of similarities, both are seduced under extenuating circumstances by a couple of temptresses, and are forever "raping home" the women of the Sabines.

Sabine leads both authors to Sabina, the name of Mr. Wilder's housekeeper, who has been "raped home" by Mr. Antrobus from one of his war expeditions. Her prototype is the garrulous housekeeper of *Finnegans Wake*. "He raped her home," says Joyce, "Sabrine asthore, in a parakeet's cage, by dredgerous lands and devious delts." To this delicious Joycean line Mr. Wilder is apparently indebted for his rape theme and the name of the Antrobus housekeeper.

The conversation between Mrs. Antrobus and Sabina in Act I carries the lilt of the Anna Livia Plurabelle chapter, and rehearses some of its themes, notably the patience of the wife while younger love beguiles her husband; and again, the little feminine attentions lavished on the man while he broods in melancholy.

The wonderful letter which the wife of Mr. Antrobus throws into the ocean at the close of Act II—that letter which would have told him all the secrets of her woman's heart and would have revealed to him the mystery of why the universe was set in motion—is precisely the puzzling missive of *Finnegans Wake*, tossed into the sea, buried in the soil, ever-awaited, ever half-found, ever reinterpreted, misinterpreted, multifariously over-and-under interpreted, which continually twinkles, with its life-riddle, through every page of Joyce's work.

In Mr. Wilder's play, the wife's name is Maggy—which is one of her names in *Finnegans Wake*. She has borne innumerable children—again see *Finnegans Wake*. Her daughter aspires to powder and rouge and fancies herself in silks (*Finnegans Wake*). The two sons, Cain and Abel, the abominated and the cherished, supply a fratricidal battle-theme that throbs through the entire play, precisely as it does in *Finnegans Wake*. Cain in both works is a peeping-tom and publisher of forbidden secrets. In Mr. Wilder's work he spies on and speaks out about the love-makings in the beach cabana. In Joyce's, he tattles the whole story of the love life of his parents.

The ingenious and very amusing scene at the close of Act I in which Tallulah Bankhead turns to the audience and begs for wood—chairs, bric-a-brac, anything at all—with which to feed the fire that will preserve humanity during the approaching ice-age, is a clever re-rendering of a passage in *Finnegans Wake*. In Joyce's work, when elemental catastrophe has almost annihilated mankind, the heroine goes about gathering into her knapsack various odds and ends, to be reanimated by the fire of life. As Joyce puts it: "She'll loan a vesta (*i.e.*, borrow a light), and hire some peat and sarch the shores her cockles to heat and she'll do all a turfwoman can . . . to puff the blaziness on." Mr. Wilder here follows Joyce's lead even to the point of having his actress borrow a light with which to ignite the preserving hearth.

There are, in fact, no end of meticulous unacknowledged copyings. At the entrance of Mr. Antrobus, for instance: his terrific banging at the door duplicates the fantastic thumpings of Joyce's hero at the gate of his own home where he is arrested for thus disturbing the peace of the whole community. The great swathing of scarfs and wrappings, which Mr. Antrobus removes when he comes in, follows the mode of Joyce's hero who is characteristically enveloped in no end of costumery. In the famous passage [in *Finnegans Wake*], HCE is seen in heaped-up attire: "caoutchouc kepi and great belt and hideinsacks and his blaufunx fustian and ironsides jackboots and Bhagafat gaiters and his rubberized inverness." Perhaps the chief difference between the protean HCE and the rigid Mr. Antrobus is revealed when the latter's wrappings are removed, leaving only a thin reminder of Joyce's grotesque folk-hero.

Throughout the work there are innumerable minor parallelisms. The razzing which Mr. Antrobus endures at the Shriner's Convention repeats the predicament of H.C. Earwicker throughout Book II, Chapter III. "The Royal Divorce" theme of *Finnegans Wake* reappears in the wish of Mr. Antrobus to be divorced from his wife. Neither of the heroes achieves his end; the wish itself being liquidated by catastrophe. The fortune-teller in Act II plays the role of Joyce's heroine, A.L.P., who assigns to all at the Masquerade the tokens of their fate. Later Mr. Wilder's gypsy coaches the seductress of Mr. Antrobus, just as "Grandma Grammar" in *Finnegans Wake* teaches Isabelle how to "decline and conjugate" young men. Trivia-wise, the key-word "commodius" occurs in the second line of *Finnegans Wake* and within the first two minutes of *The Skin of Our Teeth*. Finally, at the end of Mr. Wilder's play, the Hours pass across the stage intoning sublime instructions. This is a device conspicuous both in *Ulysses* and in *Finnegans Wake*. Many further similarities could be cited.

It is a strange performance that Mr. Wilder has turned in. Is he hoaxing us? On the one hand, he gives no credit to his source, masking it with an Olsen and Johnson technique. On the other hand, he makes no attempt to conceal his borrowings, emphasizing them rather, sometimes even stressing details which with a minimum of ingenuity he could have suppressed or altered. But if puzzlement strikes us here, it grows when we consider the critics—those literary advisors who four years ago dismissed *Finnegans Wake* as a literary abortion not worth the modern reader's time, yet today hail with rave-notices its Broadway reaction. The banquet was rejected but the Hellzapoppin's scrap that fell from the table they clutch to their bosom. Writes Alexander Woollcott, "Thornton Wilder's dauntless and heartening comedy stands head and shoulders above anything ever written for our stage." And why not, since in inception and detail the work springs from that "dauntless and heartening" genius, James Joyce!

Editor's note: *When Campbell and Robinson wrote their first article on the similarities between* The Skin of Our Teeth *and* Finnegans Wake, *they had only seen Wilder's play in the theater. After the book version of the play was published, they were more easily able to study it for similarities to Joyce's novel. In this second article, published two months after the first, their disapproval verges on outrage.*

"There are certain charges that ought not to be made, and I think I may add, ought not to be allowed to be made" (*The Skin of Our Teeth*).

"There are certain statements which ought not to be, and one should like to hope to be able to add, ought not to be allowed to be made" (*Finnegans Wake*).

Several weeks ago we made charges. We indicated a relationship between Thornton Wilder's current Broadway play, *The Skin of Our Teeth,* and that big black book, *Finnegans Wake.* Our first article, based on a single evening at the play, no more than broached the problem of Mr. Wilder's indebtedness to James Joyce. But now the appearance of the play in book form[1] offers abundant evidence that Mr. Wilder not only vigorously adapted *Finnegans Wake* to the Broadway temper, but also intended that someone, somewhere, someday, should recognize his deed for what it is.

The author had good reason to expect that this would not happen immediately. He realized fully that *Finnegans Wake* has not yet been assimilated by the larger public, and that the chances of explicit protest during the run of the play were slight. For in Joyce's work the themes are multidimensional and queerly interwoven, developing bit by bit throughout the obscure text. Even the studious eye is baffled by their intricacy. Mr. Wilder, having mastered the elaborate web, has selected a few structural strands, reduced them in size and weight, and presented them, neatly crocheted to box-office taste. Many of the Joyce-Wilder correspondences are so subtle and extended that it would require a vast wall for their exhibition. Nevertheless, within the compass of a brief article it is possible to present a series of eye-openers even to the most languid observer.

These correspondences amount to much more than a mere sharing of great and constant human themes.

1. *The Skin of Our Teeth,* A Play in Three Acts. By Thornton Wilder. New York: Harper & Bros. 1942. 142 pp. $2.

Character by character, Act by Act, unmistakable re-renderings are evident. Both works have for setting, modern suburban homes not yet detached from the archaic past. The fathers of both families are about forty-five years old; they have both just survived election campaigns, during which certain charges have been made against their character—charges indignantly denied, yet not ill-founded. Mr. Antrobus pinches servant girls when he meets them in a dark corridor; H.C.E., too, is guilty of ungentlemanly conduct with maidservants. And they both indulge in extramarital sex adventures.

Such philanderings, it may be objected, are the common stuff of literature. But in *Finnegans Wake* and *The Skin of Our Teeth* the circumstances which surround them are *H*orrendous, *C*haracteristic, and *E*special. Mark what happens directly upon the husbands' stumbling into sin:—a thunder clap is heard. Barely has Antrobus entered the cabana with the seductress, barely has H.C.E. entered the bushes, when the thunder clap resounds and the hurricane signals go up. In both works this omen is a pronouncement of God's judgment on erring man, soon to be followed by deluge. The heroes' self-apologetic radio broadcasts to the world, describing their statesmanlike contributions to humanity, along with the worlds which they celebrate, dissolve in the engulfing catastrophe.

It is not enough to fob off this complex of themes, this curious telescoping of Adam and Noah, as "something out of Genesis." Quaintly enough, this merging of patriarchs does not occur in the Bible. It does occur, however, in *Finnegans Wake*—and now in *The Skin of Our Teeth*. Furthermore, Genesis 4 relates that the first son of Adam was Cain, the second Abel. But Joyce reverses this order in *Finnegans Wake;* so, oddly enough, does Wilder. Is our Broadway playwright deriving his themes from the Hebrew or the Irish?

Mr. Wilder's maid-seductress, Sabina, assumes the traits, at one time or another, of all the temptress masks of *Finnegans Wake.* She is the servant girl, fond of movies, the Napoleonic *fille du regiment*, the worn out soubrette, the popular beauty, the captive "raped home from her Sabine hills [all as in *Finnegans Wake*]. With Joyce she is "the rainbow girl": Sabina's costume in Act I suggests the colors of the rainbow. In *Finnegans Wake,* too, all these seductress traits play over the basic personality of a gossipacious maid.

The role of maid-temptress is counterbalanced by the wife-mother, whose function it is to rebuild and preserve the life fires which, through Sabina, have gone out. In the play, as in the book, the wife borrows the light with which she kindles the hearth; even further, she borrows the light from a character who is called the Postman in the Joyce work, and in the Wilder work, Telegraph Boy. In her speeches she recalls the times when there were "no weddings" (F.W., ST.). One of her manifestations in *Finnegans Wake* is a mother hen; as Joyce puts it, "she just feels she was kind of born to lay and love eggs." Mr. Antrobus calls *his* wife a "broken down old weather hen." The umbrella that the wife carries through Wilder's Act II is the famous umbrella of *Finnegans Wake.* Mrs. Antrobus re-echoes Mrs. Earwicker's railings against the candidate and scandal-mongers who opposed her husband in the election.

The great letter that she throws into the sea is precisely the letter of *Finnegans Wake,* thrown away under identical circumstances. (Mr. Wilder's description of this letter is the most sensitive, most complete, most convincing interpretation yet to appear of this great Joycean theme.) The divorce which threatens the Antrobus household is the Royal Divorce of *Finnegans Wake.* The circumstances which postpone the divorce, and forever will postpone it, are those of *Finnegans Wake.* And again, as in *Finnegans Wake,* the mother's love for the evil, rejected Cain reconciles the male antagonisms within the family. With these parallels and the many more, it is not surprising that Mrs. Antrobus's name is Maggie,—written "Maggy" in *Finnegans Wake.*

So much for character comparisons; now for chronology. Skillfully and without essential dislocation, Mr. Wilder has adapted the four books of *Finnegans Wake* to the exigencies of a three-act play. Both works are composed in the form of a circle. Book I of *Finnegans Wake* and Act I of the play summon up the deepest past—the glacial age, dinosaurs, and mammoths (Joyce mentions both), as well as the dawn inventions of man—the alphabet, mechanics, and brewing. Book II and Act II take place in the present. Wilder's Act II is based specifically upon Book II, Section 3, of *Finnegans Wake;* Wilder simply transplants Joyce's Irish-tavern bacchanal to an Atlantic City convention. The last book of *Finnegans Wake* and the last Act of the play treat of the world's brave re-beginnings, following almost total catastrophe; they do not conclude, but circle back again to the start of all.

It is Book III of *Finnegans Wake* which would at first appear to have been omitted. But no. We find that this material has been telescoped retrospectively into the recitals of Mr. Antrobus in Act III, when he rehearses the fine ideals which he broodingly cherished during the years of struggle and war. These broodings and their return to the realities of peace correspond to H.C.E.'s dream for a future ideal and its dissolution into workaday fact. We cannot praise too highly what Mr. Wilder has here achieved in the way of re-creative interpretation. From these passages in his play a light goes back over great and very obscure sections of *Finnegans Wake.*

If the major correspondence are inescapable, minor similarities are numberless. Open the work to any page, and echoes vibrate from all directions. Some of them are highly esoteric and it is not improbable that Mr. Wilder is giving the wink of the fraternity to any Finnegan fan who may chance to be in the theatre. For instance, the play opens with an announcement that the sun arose at 6:32 a.m. Why precisely 32? This number, of all possible digits, is one of the ubiquitous puzzlers throughout the Wake: it appears during the course of the book some forty times in various combinations. Directly following the sunrise, we are shown three scrubwomen who have found Adam and Eve's wedding ring in the X Theatre. This literally reeks of Finnegan. No less than a dozen connotations spring immediately to mind: the scrubwoman theme, the entr'acte-scavenger theme, the "found article" theme, the ring theme, the wedding theme, the Phoenix Theatre theme, the "X" theme-complex (Xmas, Criss-Cross, Crucifixion-Resurrection, Crossbones, Crass-keys, XXX kisses, ex-wife, etc.), the Adam and Eve theme, etc.

An early stage direction bids Sabina to dust Mr. Antrobus's chair "including the under side." In Mr. Earwicker's tavern the man-of-all-work "dusts the both sides of the seats of the bigslaps." In Act I, in his conversation with the fish, Mr. Antrobus leans over the bowl and says, "How've things been, eh? Keck-keck-keck." When we try to remember where we have heard "keck" before, we recall the "Brekkek Kekkek" of the Aristophanes frog chorus in the diluvian passage of *Finnegans Wake.* In *The Skin of Our Teeth* "Keck" undergoes further Joycean development by appearing five times in the speeches of Esmeralda, fortune teller, who is called "Mrs. Croaker" by the convention delegates.

But why should Mr. Antrobus give special attention to a fish? Well, the fish is H.C.E.'s totem animal, as well as the giant Finn's Salmon of Knowledge.

Wilder's little girl, like Joyce's, is papa's darling, his "little star." Mr. Antrobus is revived from a mood of most desperate melancholy on hearing that she has recited Wordsworth's "The Star" in school. In *Finnegans Wake*, one of the daughter's principal manifestations is Stella (Stella—star) who revives life interest in the melancholy old man. When questioned by Mr. Antrobus, the daughter gives the exact dimensions of the ocean—a precocious knowledge suggestive of her "ocean origin" in *Finnegans Wake*.

To heap up resemblances: The message delivered by Mr. Wilder's Telegraph Boy has come by a wildly circuitous route, suggesting the peregrinations of the famous Finnegan missive. The children are called "little smellers" by Mr. Antrobus; the phrase "this little smeller" is remembered from *Finnegans Wake*. Among the refugees of the end of Act I, four old men, Doctor, Professor, Moses, and Homer, predominate; these are certainly the Four Old Men among the frequenters of Mr. Earwicker's hostel. The Antrobus inventions of beer brewing, alphabet, and mechanics are precisely those of the hero in *Finnegans Wake*.

Mr. Wilder is a man who has entered an uninventoried treasure cave and who emerges with a pouch full of sample sparklers. Only the lapidary who has himself paid a secret visit to the wonder-hoard is in a position to gasp at the authentic Joycean glitter of Mr. Wilder's re-settings.

As yet, Captain Wilder has not deigned to make public comment. But in the play itself he very cryptically pronounces as harsh an evaluation of his work as will ever be made. This pronouncement comes in Act I of *The Skin of Our Teeth*, when Mr. Antrobus comes home with his epochal invention, the wheel, which his son seizes with delight. Playing with the wheel, the son says: "Papa, you could put a chair on this." To which the father replies, broodingly: "Ye-e-s, any booby can fool with it now,—but I thought of it first."

The wheel is James Joyce's circular book of cyclewheeling history, "the Book of Doublends Jined"; Mr. Wilder has cleverly fixed a chair to it, wherein the public can ride.

Comparisons Between *Finnegans Wake* and *The Skin of Our Teeth* Have Been Exaggerated

Donald Haberman

Donald Haberman began his book *The Plays of Thornton Wilder: A Critical Study* as his doctoral thesis at Wilder's alma mater, Yale University. In this excerpt from his book, Haberman examines the relationship between *The Skin of Our Teeth* and *Finnegans Wake*. Although Haberman acknowledges that the Irish James Joyce was undoubtedly a rich source of inspiration, there were many others—including those who had originally inspired Joyce. What Wilder brought was his own way of looking at life; what resulted, Haberman declares, was not a bowdlerized version of *Finnegans Wake* designed for mass consumption, but a new and essentially American work.

Although the emphasis in his plays is on the narration, the sequence of events, Wilder has recognized the need of his audience for a story of some sort. The audience may create the story themselves, but Wilder has provided the clues. Any understanding of Wilder's style will depend, therefore, on the nature of those clues.

The anecdote in Wilder's plays is subservient to its meaning, but Wilder does not spin out ideas or philosophic systems. His abiding interest lies in human nature and its story. To explain what he intended by providing a work for the theater with significance, Wilder told the *Paris Review* interviewer:

> All the greatest dramatists, except the very greatest *one*, have precisely employed the stage to convey a moral or religious point of view concerning the action. . . .

I get around this difficulty by what may be an impertinence on my part. By believing that the moralizing intention resided in the authors as a convention of their times—usually, a social convention so deeply buried in the author's mode of thinking that it seemed to him to be inseparable from creation. . . . I say they injected a didactic intention in order to justify to themselves and to their audiences the exhibition of pure experience.[1]

Wilder is not a pamphleteer; his interest is not in social reform. For him the theater is the place where physical and emotional experience is arranged as effectively and precisely as possible.

In the introduction he wrote for Richard Beer-Hoffmann's *Jaakobs Traum,* Wilder explained how myth might resolve the differences between "didactic intention" and the "exhibition of pure experience."

A myth passing from oral tradition into literature, moves most congenially into poetry and particularly into the poetic drama. Even the most rationalistic reader consents to receive as given the elements of the supernatural and the incredible that are involved in these ancient stories. Their validity rests on the general ideas they contain. . . . The characters whom we have endowed with the life of significant ideas must be endowed with a different kind of life from the realistic—that of the recognizable quotidian.[2]

Characters from myth must be provided with a daily living that is ordinary and common to the audience. The advantage of employing a myth as the basis of a literary work is that it is already equipped with the substance of significant ideas. The anthropologist's and the psychologist's explanations of myth are dismissed as trivial and determined by detail of historical time and geographical place. More important to the artist is the problem of self-knowledge—individual and racial—which is enduring. The persistent elements of myth

are questions and not answers in regard to the human situation. In the majority of cases the questions seem to have to do with the mind disengaging itself from the passions of finding its true position in the presence of the established authorities, human or divine. They are concretizations of man's besetting preoccupation with the mind and mind's struggle to know itself; and each retelling requires that some answer be furnished to the question that infuses every part of the story.[3]

It is not sufficient to provide the myth with psychology or ordinary rational behavior. No amount of contemporary

1. Malcolm Cowley, ed., *Writers at Work* (New York, 1958), p. 109. 2. Richard Beer-Hoffmann, *Jacob's Dream* (New York, 1946), p. xvi. 3. *Ibid.,* p. xiii.

detail superimposed on the myth can make it significant. Its modernity must be inherent in its story, and the questions it raises must be answered, not finally for all time, but within the artist's comprehension of the world around him. His retelling will be judged by the questions he understands in the myth and the answers he provides to them, his separation of the eternal from the merely ephemeral.

MYTH FITS WILDER'S VIEW OF THE THEATER

Myth is well fitted to Wilder's idea of the theater, for it is peculiarly equipped to convey a generalized statement about human beings who seem themselves to be individualized. The writer need not bother to provide the characters of myth with details irrelevant to his idea in order to make the characters real. They are already in possession of a reality resulting from their existence throughout time. Neither does the plot concern the writer especially. Of greater importance is the large idea he sees illustrated in the story that is there. If, as Wilder believes, the anecdote matters only insofar as it illustrates that idea, then myth is the ideal anecdote because its general outlines are already known in some way to the audience. A myth is available to everyone. It is, as Wilder wrote in an essay on Joyce, "the dreaming soul of the race telling its story." Furthermore, he wrote that the "retelling of them on every hand occurs because they whisper a validation—they isolate and confer a significance."[4]

Wilder has really always used a myth as the anecdote for his plays. The story of Emily's return from the dead is not a classical myth, but Wilder had used it earlier in *The Woman of Andros* as though it were. Chrysis recounts it as a myth, and its adaptability to retelling is further evidence of its mythic quality. *The Merchant of Yonkers* is not a real myth either, but since its story is based on other works of literature, it is regarded by Wilder as a kind of myth. He, like Pound and Eliot, uses the writings of others as though they were part of the great body of ideas available to the entire human group, or in other words a myth: "Every novel for sale in a railway station is the dreaming soul of the human race telling its story."[5] *The Skin of Our Teeth* does use myth; furthermore, it employs history as though it were myth. The entire play is provided with coherence and additional mean-

4. Thornton Wilder, "Joyce and the Modern Novel," *A James Joyce Miscellany* (n.p., 1957), p. 15. 5. *Ibid.*

ing by its use of what Wilder would call a recent retelling of a myth, of many myths, *Finnegans Wake.*

CHARGES OF PLAGIARISM

Almost immediately after the opening of *The Skin of Our Teeth* two articles[6] by Joseph Campbell and Henry Morton Robinson in the *Saturday Review of Literature* linked the play with *Finnegans Wake.* The intent of these two men is not very clear; the tone they assumed, however, seems from this distance of time inexcusable, and a subsequent essay[7] by Robinson made evident his feeling, at least, that Wilder had been dishonest.

Campbell and Robinson wavered between assuming that the play was some sort of literary prank, the fun being able to recognize it, and stating baldly that it was something shoddy masquerading as first-rate. Perhaps this divided attitude indicates a division in the writers. Whatever their intent, when readers of the *Saturday Review of Literature* concluded that Wilder was a plagiarist, neither writer denied that the charge had been their idea in writing the articles. Perhaps the editorial policy of the magazine was at fault. The play, as a result of the two articles, for a while acquired the reputation of being at best unoriginal and derivative and at worst the unsavory work of thievery and plagiarism. Even today, reviews of its performance or comments on it display an uneasiness that can be traced to the *Saturday Review of Literature* articles.

Campbell and Robinson had been working on their *Skeleton Key to Finnegans Wake* and were in an unusually favorable position to recognize Wilder's debt to Joyce. Although they amassed all kinds of evidence to demonstrate the debt, they did not describe, or were unwilling to recognize, its precise nature. *The Skin of Our Teeth* is not, in fact, a dramatization of *Finnegans Wake,* as Edmund Wilson, who was not enthusiastic about the play, immediately recognized.[8]

Wilder never directly answered the two articles, which after all amounted to an attack, though he was painfully aware of them. His few simple and deceptively ingenuous remarks

---

6. Joseph Campbell and Henry Morton Robinson, "The Skin of Whose Teeth?," *Saturday Review of Literature,* XXV (December 19, 1942), 3–4, and "The Skin of Whose Teeth?: Part II," *Saturday Review of Literature,* XXVI (February 13, 1943), 16–19. 7. Henry Morton Robinson, "The Curious Case of Thornton Wilder," *Esquire,* XLVII (March, 1957), 70–71, 124, 125, 126. 8. Edmund Wilson, "The Antrobuses and The Earwickers," *Nation,* CXVI (January 30, 1943), 167f.

about Joyce and *The Skin of Our Teeth* have not supported his position very much. In 1948 he told an interviewer:

> I embedded one phrase of "Finnegans Wake" into the text as a salute and a bow of homage. . . .
>
> Sabina mockingly defending her employer, Mr. Antrobus who is also Adam and Everyman, says, "There are certain charges that ought not to be made and, I think I may say, ought not to be allowed to be made." This speech, with its feeble cadence and insecure indignation, is a wonderful example of Joyce's miraculous ear.
>
> "There are no other lines from Joyce?"
>
> "None," said Mr. Wilder.[9]

This clears up what was never in doubt really. The disturbing accusation of Campbell and Robinson was not that Wilder lifted lines from *Finnegans Wake,* but that he had adapted Joyce's inspiration and vision. They wrote, "Important plot elements, characters, devices of presentation, as well as major themes and many of the speeches, are directly and frankly imitated."[10] Wilder's statement is no answer to this kind of attack.

OTHER SOURCES

It is important first to be reminded that many of the devices and themes that Wilder found in his reading of Joyce he had come across earlier. The notion of circular time, for example, is as easily discovered in Vico's *Scienza Nuova,* where Joyce himself found it. But Gertrude Stein also had been fascinated with the possibilities in this idea, and Dreiser, a still earlier enthusiasm of Wilder's, was too.

In Dreiser's *Laughing Gas* a Doctor Vatabeel undergoes an operation which routinely should be simple, but grows more dangerously complicated as the play progresses. The anesthetic used is laughing gas, hence the title of the play; and it is while under the effect of the gas that the vision of repeated existing is revealed to Vatabeel. He dumbly considers: "In older worlds I have been, worlds like this. I have done this same thing. Society has done all the things it has done over and over."[11]

Vatabeel is pictured as an "endlessly serviceable victim—an avatar,"[12] with progress existing merely as an empty illusion. The urge to life, however, seems to work in him almost in spite of himself, as though it were a reflex action,

9. Robert van Gelder, "Interview with a Best-Selling Author: Thornton Wilder," *Cosmopolitan,* CXXIV (April, 1948), 120. 10. "The Skin of Whose Teeth?," p. 3. 11. Theodore Dreiser, *Plays of the Natural and the Supernatural* (New York, 1916), p. 107. 12. *Ibid.,* p. 109.

responding in defiance of his will to the stimulus of the operation. Various Voices urge him to try; he "senses some vast, generic, undecipherable human need."[13] At the same time the rhythm of the universe pounds a "sense of derision of indifference, of universal terror and futility."[14] Demyophon, one of the spirits of the Universe, tells him: "It has no meaning! Over and over! Round and round! . . . What you do now you will do again. And there is no explanation. You are so eager to live—to do it again. Do you not see the humor of that?"[15] And Vatabeel wakes from the gas laughing.

In Dreiser's grotesque play are two ideas that have remained with Wilder throughout his writing career. First and most apparent is the circular and repetitive nature of experience. Second and closely allied with the first is the existence in the individual, race, world, or evolution simultaneously of all experience. Vatabeel not only endlessly repeats experience; he is its avatar as well.

Of course, *Laughing Gas* is just barely literature, and Joyce's novel is one of the great if secret books of our time. Wilder, however, is one of the comparatively few men who have come close to deciphering the mysteries of *Finnegans Wake*, for he has spent hours and hours of his time, especially just before and after the war, reading it, and he possesses the knowledge and the languages to overcome its most obvious difficulties. In 1949 Wilder said at the Goethe Centennial celebration at Aspen, Colorado, that Joyce demonstrates that all the world at all times is one. He continued to say that Joyce did not use the work of others for "allusion, illustration, or ornament," but for "ambience."[16] Here, I think, Wilder has described his own attitude toward the work of Joyce and all his other "sources" as well.

"MAKE IT NEW"

The American writer has the disadvantage of being dependent on Europe (usually) for his culture and history, for the United States has provided relatively little of either commodity. Yet the artist requires both, and Henry James, Pound, Eliot, and Hemingway, to name only a very few, are American writers who made good use of what Europe had to offer without losing their distinctive American spirit.[17]

13. *Ibid.*, p. 110. 14. *Ibid.* 15. *Ibid*, p. 112. 16. Thornton Wilder, "World Literature and the Modern Mind," in Arnold Bergstraesser, ed., *Goethe and the Modern Age* (Chicago, 1950), p. 218. 17. Norman Holmes Pearson, "The American Novelist and the Uses of Europe," *Some American Studies* (Kyoto, 1964).

Wilder has made just such use of Joyce, but he has each time heeded Ezra Pound's command to Make It New, for Wilder learned from Ezra Pound how to master the literary as well as the historic past.[18] *Finnegans Wake* provided for Wilder's play a myth of the historical and cultural environment which created America. Its advantages to Wilder may be summed up in his definition of the kind of story a myth is.

First, its "historical authenticity is so far irrelevant as to permit to the narrator an assumption of omniscience in regard to what took place."[19] The writer need not waste any effort establishing the truth of his story. No matter how fantastic the events, they are accepted by the audience as having happened exactly as the writer reports them.

Secondly, a myth is a story "whose antiquity and popular diffusion confer upon it an authority which limits the degree of variation that may be employed in its retelling."[20] The major outlines of the story must be retained to satisfy the audience's pleasure in recognizing the familiar.

Finally, a myth is a story "whose subject matter is felt to have a significance which renders each retelling a contribution to the received ideas of the entire community to which in a very real sense it belongs."[21] Here is the most difficult task for the writer. He must demonstrate his originality, not in the plot, but in the meaning. He must create a significance that does not overstep the limitations of the events that are given, but a significance that is new and contemporary.

18. Ezra Pound is one of the two modern American writers whom Wilder admires and to whom he feels indebted. See Cowley, *Writers at Work*, p. 115. 19. Beer-Hofmann, *Jacob's Dream*, p. xi. 20. *Ibid.* 21. *Ibid.*, p. xii.

CAMPBELL AND ROBINSON WERE MISTAKEN

It is a serious mistake to assume, as Campbell and Robinson did, that Wilder's play is a rehash of Joyce's novel. Readers of Virgil who come to the *Aeneid* after Homer are inevitably disappointed in Aeneas and utterly fail to understand the Latin epic if they demand another Achilles or Odysseus. Just so puzzled and irritated were Campbell and Robinson when they did not find in Antrobus an exact copy of H.C. Earwicker. In spite of all the parallels between *Finnegans Wake* and *The Skin of Our Teeth* that Campbell and Robinson uncovered, it is careless to conclude, as they did, that Wilder merely collected and catalogued Joyce's discoveries into an adaptation suitable to the Broadway temper. That he had studied and comprehended Joyce's work is certain; but he also succeeded in pervading the whole of his play with his own optimistic and peculiarly American vision of the human animal and his experience through time.

It is not simple patriotism that locates Antrobus and his family in New Jersey. No matter if he is Adam or Noah or Everybody, he is America's version of Man, and unlike Joyce's heroes, he is not determined by his environment, whether it be cultural, physical, or moral. Antrobus is eternally extricating himself from his "ambience" or reinterpreting it or literally changing it. When the American confronts an ice age, he will invent a more efficient way to heat his house.

In 1928 Wilder told André Maurois, "In the whole of the world's literature there are only seven or eight great subjects. By the time of Euripides they had all been dealt with already, and all one can do is to pick them up again. . . . There is nothing new that a writer can hope to bring except a certain way of looking at life."[22] Wilder brought to the myths of *Finnegans Wake* precisely another way of interpreting them. He saw in Joyce's work another version of the Europe that has been so important to the American writer. Perhaps, as Professor Pearson suggests,[23] the actual experience of Europe has become too commonplace for American writers, but the secondary or literary experience is still available. Through Joyce's novel, Wilder reinterpreted Europe for the American. Antrobus is free to escape—though with the skin of his teeth only—and create a new independent future. It is more than

22. André Maurois, *A Private Universe*, tr. Hamish Miles (New York, 1932), p. 39. 23. "The American Novelist and the Uses of Europe," p. 18.

mere chance, in the light of what the Old World has always dreamed of the United States and perhaps during World War II more realistically expected from it, that *The Skin of Our Teeth* should have presented for a destroyed and to all appearances utterly debilitated Europe a promise for the future. Wilder's play is unquestionably an original work. It portrays the mythic American cheerfully and energetically progressing through a mythic Western civilization.

THE RELIGIOUS HERO

That the American has no sense of tragedy is perhaps a national flaw, but as Wilder has noted, it is just as surely a major source of national energy. The American has created a new kind of hero, distinct from the tragic hero, and this new hero offers a challenge to American writers for the theater. Using Abraham as an example, Kierkegaard described just such a hero, calling him the religious hero. . . .

Ethical standards may exist, but for the religious hero they are meaningless because he does not act for others, except as he acts for himself. The usual motives of the tragic hero are absent. . . . For [Wilder] the religious hero is the person who is most intensely alive, the person most intimately related with his everyday existence. The divine is simply that which is unknowable, and it is the unknowable that clarifies everyday living by forcing attention to it. This understanding is not unchristian, but it is more general than most traditional theology would allow.

Kierkegaard wrote also that the "tragic hero accomplishes his act at a definite instant in time."[24] The religious hero's act is performed in "an absolute relation to the absolute," which is not so impersonal as it might first seem, for he is justified by "being the particular individual."[25] The connection between what Wilder learned from Gertrude Stein and what he learned from Kierkegaard is probably most clearly perceptible here. The freedom of Kierkegaard's religious hero is the rootlessness described by Gertrude Stein as the moving in all directions, the absence of a beginning, middle, and end, characteristic of America and the Bible. It is Wilder's "abstract" American and another way of describing the validity of the individual in the face of all the millions who have lived, who are living, and who will live.

24. S. Kierkegaard, *Fear and Trembling,* tr. Walter Lowrie (Princeton, 1941), p. 91.
25. *Ibid.,* p. 93

The success of Wilder's theater, which has not been recognized because every attempt has been made to measure it
against the old standards, is, in fact, that he has helped create new standards. Whether or not we derive pleasure from
the theater he has so carefully developed will probably
depend on whether or not we are happy about the political,
social, and intellectual changes that have resulted in our
time and country.

Archetypal Characters in *The Skin of Our Teeth*

Helmut Papajewski, translated by John Conway

The Skin of Our Teeth, which opened during World War II, uses archetypal characters to explore the question of whether humanity would change in the wake of the devastation it had brought upon itself, writes Helmut Papajewski, author of a German study on Wilder's works. Papajewski examines the major characters—the Antrobus family and Sabina—and the complex links to their biblical and mythical forerunners.

On October 15, 1942, in the little Shubert Theater in New Haven, Connecticut, *The Skin of Our Teeth* received its first performance. This out-of-town premiere was followed on November 18 by the New York opening at the Plymouth Theater. Wilder's new play—with its title indicating alarm, hope, and resignation—was an outgrowth of world events and literary experiences since his last work. The Second World War had entered its fourth year, and for almost a year America had been actively engaged. Wilder does not pose any specifically political questions concerning this war, but directs his attention once again to the anthropological-ethical problem connected with it: If man survives this war too, will he fundamentally change his ways? There were many political programs during this war, but Wilder had experienced too much disillusionment after World War One—when he was already at the age of awareness—for him to place very much credence in the new program; and he had too clear an idea of man's limited possibilities and the chance of relapse to be able to share the renewed easy optimism. Antrobus speaks of all this in down-to-earth language in Act Three: "When you're at war you think about a better life; when you're at peace you think about a more comfortable one." With all their stress on "reality," the politicians were bound to build their grand designs in a vacuum, because they did not take into account the really decisive thing, the world's anthropological substructure. . . .

Viewed in relation to previous drama, the Wilder play differs in the manner of its division into three acts, and in a way also in the kind of plot as given by the title. The title implies that man once again escapes from his current plight and that his personal behavior approximates that of characters in a comedy—a comedy, to be sure, with metaphysical overtones rather than a straight comedy of definite time and place.

The play's three acts do not represent one continuous action. Each culminates in a great world catastrophe: the Ice Age, the Deluge, and the World War. Out of each catastrophe man finds his way by dint of his enthusiasm for a new beginning, without fundamentally changing his ways, for the evil which drove him into the catastrophe remains immanent in him.

THE TWO ASPECTS OF MAN

Thus man is seen under two aspects: as a creature who is delivered up to these catastrophes, and as a creature who lives in the self-contained unit of the family. Wilder sets forth both of these aspects at the very beginning. In place of the usual prologue there are lantern-slide showings by the announcer, which are meant to give a graphic idea of the oppressive cold. This "prelude" alludes at the same time to the crisis within the family: a wedding ring is found with the inscription, "To Eve from Adam."

From these lantern-slide showings Wilder shifts to the Antrobus family, which has to cope with the threatening Ice Age. It is a deranged and topsy-turvy world that is presented to us. In the warmest month, August, the severest frost prevails. The walls of the house rise, sink, and lean to one side. The dinosaur lives with man, at one point drolly taking its place with Mrs. Antrobus and the children in a triangular tableau reminiscent of Raphael. The alphabet is invented, and the fact is announced by telegram. Antrobus discovers the arithmetic significance of tens, though the course of the proceedings shows that the concept has long been part of the currency of human thought. Instability appears to be raised to the level of a principle, and anachronism displaces the normal time pattern.

There is plenty of fun with this hyper-baroque theater. Many over-serious playgoers, on the other hand, have been irritated by such "nonsense." The sense of what Wilder is up to is disclosed only when it is remembered that the real world of our life in the here-and-now was strongly called into question: the reality of this world had proved to be only a seeming reality. . . .

In our everyday life we are not in a position to penetrate the sense-deception of the world around us. Wilder returns to this idea, in the course of representing each hour of the twenty-four with a philosopher, at the ninth hour in the evening, represented by Spinoza:

> After experience had taught me that the common occurrences of daily life are vain and futile; and I saw that all the objects of my desire and fear were in themselves nothing good nor bad save insofar as the mind was affected by them; I at length determined to search out whether there was something truly good and communicable to man.

Spinoza with nine o'clock represents the beginning of the intellectually reflective hours of the night. Before being followed by Plato and Aristotle, he called attention to the meaning of the "common occurrences of daily life." But what a role these "common occurrences" have played in Wilder's dramas! *Our Town* was completely geared to them—only to lead them finally *ad absurdum* in the life of Emily. Seen from this standpoint, then, *The Skin of Our Teeth* is a consistent continuation of the small-town play. Of course it does not begin with the "occurrences," not even when in the course of the First Act the view narrows from the wide-angle lens of the "announcer" down to the family circle.

A Composite Family Tree

This Antrobus family lives in a dual system of categories, the one being in terms of nature and natural catastrophe, and the other being religious-eschatological. The name Antrobus is itself a hint of this; one thinks of the Greek word *anthropos.* Wilder represents him as the Chief of the mammals and president of their assembly. Antrobus speaks of the beginning of life billions of years ago, and he even gives a presentation of the polygenetic development of man.

But beside this there is another family tree and another chronology: here the span is not billions of years, but the 4,000 to 5,000 years of world history according to Biblical tradition. In this family tree, Antrobus becomes the Old Testament Adam, both figures merging to form a composite. From the statement of the "announcer," the provenance of Anthropos-Adam is clear: "He comes of very old stock and made his way up from next to nothing." Following Genesis, the "announcer" continues: "It is reported that he was once a gardener, but left that situation under circumstances that have been variously reported." Antrobus is the genius who invented such things as the wheel (which is not expressly mentioned in the Bible); but he is also the inventor of beer, and this suggests the Biblical parallel Noah.

This parallel becomes still clearer with the events of the Second Act. When the Deluge comes, Antrobus takes pairs of all species of animal aboard the Ark, two by two, and thus helps to save creation. All animals are represented, even the famous Biblical snake to which Gladys calls attention while embarking.

RACIAL AND RELIGIOUS PARENTAGE

The Biblical parentage is not limited to one meaning or one person, but, just as the natural racial parentage reflected all vital stages of development, so also the religious parentage has—if not all—many essential features in itself. Among these is the wounding of Antrobus that causes his limp: it is the wound he received in the fight over the absolute, the wound of Jacob. Sabina at one point characterizes him with mingled mockery and approval: ". . . An excellent husband and father, a pillar of the church, and has all the best interests of the community at heart. Of course, every muscle goes tight every time he passes a policeman."

All this sounds very bourgeois, but the analogies point beyond: Antrobus is not only the first man, Adam, but also the progenitor of the people and guardian of the community, Abraham. The Biblical analogy probably extends to David, whose sins of the flesh are reflected in Antrobus. It is interesting to see how the analogy is not always unequivocal. The Henry-Cain analogy is an example: Cain has killed someone with a slingshot, the typical weapon of David.

Wilder has discussed at length the use of this kind of literary technique in his lecture "Goethe and World Literature." Referring to Goethe's thesis that "national literature" now does not "say" much and that one must take into account mankind's "long memory"—Wilder is borrowing a phrase from Ortega y Gasset—Wilder takes up the subject of Goethe's employment of universal materials: "He did not shrink from anachronisms. He wedded his Faust to Helena; he grafted his Weimar on to Shiraz, the city of the Persian poet." It is not a question here of whether the examples Wilder has chosen from Goethe are, from the standpoint of tradition, entirely correct. What is much more important in the present connection is Wilder's reference to Goethe's mode of relating and integrating things of different cultures. . . .

The recourse to world literature is important for Wilder in another sense also. He sees in it the expression of the fact that man as an individual is in the millions—a view that may also have its significance in connection with his speculations about the soul's divestment of its individuality after death. . . .

HENRY-CAIN, THE EVIL ONE

From the beginning it is quite definite that Henry is Cain. Sabina gives it away at the beginning of the First Act. A tactful yet incautious question by Moses awakens Mrs. Antrobus' grief over the loss of Abel. It is she who tries again and again with her apron to rub away the mark of Cain from her son's forehead—but it remains. Cain, too, must remain. From a dramaturgic standpoint he is the recurrent type; from a metaphysical standpoint he is the Evil that must accompany man. His existence makes Antrobus despair and wish himself rid of this son who makes himself intolerable in all polite society. Evil is ordained for him as the curse of man's original Fall. Nor can it be domesticated. Wilder has included in *The Skin of Our Teeth* a number of contrast scenes by which he aims to show that man in a state of peril gives himself up to illusions. Thus we see Sabina in a bourgeois fashion doing the housework and dusting everything when the Ice Age is already close at hand. Thus we see Antrobus just before the Flood, planning to take his sweetheart to a hotel room. Above all there is the scene in which Antrobus, who should have no illusions about Cain's nature, sits at the family hearth drilling him in the multiplication table.

The essential element is the constant accompaniment of that which is evil, with which Antrobus must identify himself, as in the scene where Sabina breaks the news to him that Cain has killed the neighbors' son. At first Antrobus is extremely angry, and despite the approach of the Ice Age he wants to stamp out the life-preserving fire—on which everything constantly depends and which only Mrs. Antrobus is really competent to preserve—and in this way to put an end to everything. Then the sense of his own guilt returns: "Henry! Henry! (Puts his hand on his forehead.) Myself. All of us, we're covered with blood.". . .

Antrobus is the master of the house, who should give the family its solidarity, whereas Cain is increasingly the one without any ties, who wants no home and no solidarity. Even a total war with all its consequences cannot awake such desires in him. When Henry-Cain after the world war emerges a general from the air raid shelter, he rejects all shelter and all ties, to say nothing of order and subordination. His mother's wish that there be peace at last in the family as well as in the world, he brusquely rejects: "I don't live here. I don't belong to anybody."

Still stronger is his negation of his father: "You don't have to think I'm any relation of yours. I haven't got any father or any mother, or brothers or sisters. And I don't want any. And what's more I haven't got anybody over me; and I never will have. I'm alone, and that's all I want to be: alone." The man without any ties, the man who denies, is also the man who brooks no commandments: "Nobody can say *must* to me."

Henry-Cain is also the embodiment of the so-called new political principles, which equate youth with an unbridled striving for power. All contemporaries still remember the words, "What have they done for us?", and still more "When are you going to wake up?" Toward the play's end, however, Wilder does not see Cain as representing the revolt of youth, but as a representation of strong unreconciled evil, of whom it is said in the stage directions at the very end: "Henry appears at the edge of the scene, brooding and unreconciled, but present." When creation begins again, he is there, just as at the second Creation by Noah the serpent was also among those present.

THE TWO EVES

Among the female characters Mrs. Antrobus is Eve (Hebrew for "the maternal one") who guards the fire that keeps life. Opposed to her is Sabina as the other Eve, the temptress. Sabina appears in the play under various names which give clues to her identity. When the characters are introduced by the announcer, she is called Lily Sabina; she is also called the servant girl. She is the daughter of Lilith of Talmudic tradition; and Lilith is of the night, demonic: she is the evil female, the night-hag.

She has not come into the family by orderly process, but—as her name Sabina indicates—by rapine. In the first argument between the two main female characters of the play, Mrs. Antrobus gives the facts about Sabina's past: "O,

Sabina, I know you. When Mr. Antrobus raped you home from your Sabine hills, he did it to insult me. You were the new wife, weren't you?" But Sabina finally did not hold her place. She let the fire go out, and was demoted to the kitchen to be servant instead of guardian of the fire. In the next-to-last scene of the Third Act she says resignedly: "Kitchen! Why is it that however far I go away, I always find myself back in the kitchen?" For her, life has no other final solution than servitude.

In the Second Act it does appear for a time that her hour has come. Her name is enlarged to Sabina Fairweather, a reference to the time of her effectiveness. In crises she always fails; in fair weather she is able to achieve recognition, as when Antrobus becomes President. But it is President of a state full of illusions, where the "truth" is obtained from the fortune-teller and accomplice of prostitutes. Esmeralda the gypsy seems to have the power of regulating the action, but it is action that is altogether brittle and cannot last. The brief dream of Helen of Troy, about whom Sabina asks the fortune-teller, is finally over, and Sabina says naïvely: "I don't know why my life's always being interrupted—just when everything's going fine!" Esmeralda has just banished her to the kitchen: "Yes, go— back to the kitchen with you."

The Second Act not only marks Sabina's seduction of Mr. Antrobus and demonstrates his moral blindness in seeing in the prostitute the loved one; but also, in the Second Act, it is through Sabina that Antrobus becomes conscious of his own guilt. When he sees Gladys wearing the red stockings, the color of Man's Fall and of temptation, he realizes at once that the source of this is Sabina. His own guilt causes him to guard against his daughter's going wrong.

The four main characters—Mr. and Mrs. Antrobus, Henry, and Sabina—make up the world, in its good aspect as well as its bad. The one cannot be divorced from the other, and nothing can be made an absolute value. The human archetypes which these characters embody form the foundation on which being—for Wilder, Christian being—rests. In them Wilder's cycle of theological existence runs a full course: "The Fall as the result of sin, the dawning consciousness of what is sinful, the new beginning in excessive hope and in pride, and thereby the first beginning of a new Fall.". . .

THE LINK WITH "REALITY"

In this play Sabina is the one to whom Wilder assigns the task of establishing the link with "reality," as that term is understood by people generally. She repeatedly acts out of character. She does not understand the play or does not want to. Parts of it she does not want to play because a friend of hers is present in the theater and parts of it might shock her by recalling her own hard fate.

But Sabina's function is also that she must ironically play the play out. At one point she names the play by its title. As Miss Somerset, she says three times in the First Act: ". . . A few years ago we came through the depression by the skin of our teeth! One more tight squeeze like that and where will we be?" The audience receives a strong and sustained statement of the play's theme, but the words are in an ironical context, for this very statement is also a cue line and the prompter is unable to respond. Miss Somerset makes use of the breakdown to address herself to the audience.

Through her outbursts she establishes the link to the audience, and the stage manager has to bring her back into the action of the play. Thus the stage manager has a function somewhat the reverse of that in *Our Town*. In that play, within his technical limits, he let the people come forward; and he repeatedly bridged the gap between the transcendental area and the here-and-now. In *The Skin of Our Teeth* the transcendental is itself here, and the task of the stage manager is limited.

BREAKING CHARACTER FOR EFFECT

The startling effects are so increased in *The Skin of Our Teeth* that they bear upon the movement and the success of the play itself. Occasionally a minor character such as the telegraph boy makes a remark to this effect: "I . . . I can't do this last part very well." Antrobus too has trouble with his role. In a scene in which Sabina has created a sort of general chaos, he cannot get back on track right away. Antrobus: "Wait a minute. I can't get back into it as easily as all that."

Sabina is the one who, more than anyone else, puts everything in question. She seems to have certain intellectual difficulties. When it dawns on her that the crisis also brings the refugee problem, she briefly gives vent to her feelings. She tries to avert an ugly encounter between the angry father and the furious son by saying: "Stop! Stop! Don't play this scene," even reminding the players what happened when this scene was played in the previous evening's performance.

Sabina, the frivolous one, who in *The Skin of Our Teeth* does not see any eschatological event but only sees a threat, gives vent to her aversion to the play: "I hate this play and every word in it. As for me, I don't understand a single word of it, anyway—all about the troubles the human race has gone through, there's a subject for you."

Wilder even takes the opportunity to have Sabina make sarcastic remarks about him as a dramatist. Sabina, in a commedia dell'arte situation, had been told by the prompter to improvise something, at which she had only poor success. She now gives her opinion of the play's content, which is unclear and seems to have been insufficiently thought out: "Besides the author hasn't made up his silly mind as to whether we're all living back in caves or in New Jersey today, and that's the way it is all the way through."

A VISIBLE TREND TO UNIVERSALITY

Something of their double nature is still to be detected in the characters, their ephemeral quality bound by time and place, as well as their human universality. In the inclinations of the characters there is still the father-daughter and mother-son relationship—Maggie is concerned for Henry, Antrobus for Gladys—just as in *Our Town*. But by making the usual space and time relationships questionable from the beginning, Wilder manages to reach the sphere that encompasses the millions of living and dead. The play's entire design in this respect is anchored so firmly in the typological that in the nomenclature of persons as well as places there is a visible trend to universality, to the metaphysical comedy of types, and to the grand style.

In *The Skin of Our Teeth* there is no longer a Grover's Corners [of *Our Town*] that can be located by its degree of latitude and longitude, no Webbs and no Gibbses, but only the four basic human types, who are, to be sure, organized as a family, but whose significance is purely archetypical. Even when specific place names are still given, as in the brief listing of school, department store, etc., they are not meant to play any role in the play, but represent certain human necessities: education, divine worship, satisfaction of one's daily wants. They will remain, according to Wilder's view, as will also the primeval types of good and evil in a world of recurring catastrophes. "Oh, anyway," Sabina exclaims, "nothing matters! It'll all be the same in a hundred years." It is Sabina, too, who closes the play, shuffling the levels of reality as she refers simultaneously to herself, the audience, and humanity: "This is where you came in. We have to go on for ages and ages yet."

A Powerful Study of Humanity's Ability to Survive

David Castronovo

Wilder's jumble of theatrical styles helps support the universal themes in *The Skin of Our Teeth*, explains David Castronovo. Comparing *The Skin of Our Teeth* with *Our Town*, Castronovo declares the former play both more penetrating and more satisfying. Castronovo argues that Wilder assimilated influences from world theater, particularly the works of Pirandello and Brecht, to produce a play that simultaneously deals with everyday American life and "the churnings of the universe." Castronovo is also the author of works on Edmund Wilson and Richard Yates, and of *The English Gentleman: Images and Ideals in Literature and Society.*

Measuring Wilder's progress as a dramatist inevitably involves placing *The Skin of Our Teeth* beside *Our Town:* the works invite comparison not only because of their ambitiousness but more importantly because of strong thematic affinities. Both concern American families struggling with implacable fate and their own smallness: Emily and George and their parents and Mr. and Mrs. Antrobus and their children experience joy and dread as they contend not only with the localized social problems of American life, but more importantly with the churnings of the universe. The macrocosmic references in both plays—to planets, vast numbers, ideas that hover around mortal lives—are an unmistakable sign that Wilder remains obsessed by the ways ordinary lives in Grover's Corners or Excelsior, New Jersey, take their place in a universal design. But for all this similarity in cosmic subject matter, there is a very considerable difference in the dramatic visions of the plays. The last act of *Our Town* takes place in a graveyard—its epiphanies are tragic, but its affirmations about stars and striving are so much inauthentic rhetoric grafted onto a great play. Unfortunately for those who seek easy contrasts with *The Skin of Our Teeth,* the later play—for all its brio and broad humor—is not essentially comic, although a wide variety of comic and humorous strategies are used in the very serious, emotionally wrenching drama about the struggle to transcend the disasters of nature, human society, and the warped human self. Act III situates the family in a war-ravaged home with Gladys as an unwed mother, Henry filled with fascistic rage, and Sabina anxious to become a good self-absorbed American citizen ready for a peacetime prosperity of movies and fun. Mr. Antrobus is ready to start putting the world together again, but he is old and tired and has had many setbacks. This is hardly comic—and in its matter-of-fact look at what men and women wind up with, it is hardly the complacent vision that repelled Mary McCarthy when she reviewed the play.[1] *The Skin of Our Teeth* is not about the fat of the land: what's in view for man is grinding struggle, close calls with total destruction, and the permanent fact of human violence and selfishness.

SHATTERING DRAMATIC CONVENTIONS

This theme of human struggle and limited achievement comes to us in the form of three loosely constructed, elliptical acts. Never a writer of well-made plays, Wilder has now brought his own episodic technique to a pitch of dizzy perfection. From his *Journals* we learn that Wilder considered that he was "shattering the ossified conventions" of realistic drama in order to let his "generalized beings" emerge.[2]

Act I, set in Excelsior, New Jersey, has about as much logic and verisimilitude as a vaudeville skit. Using the Brechtian strategy of screen projections and announcements, Wilder surveys the "News Events of the World." Mostly the reports concern the extreme cold, the wall of ice moving south, and the scene in the home of George Antrobus. It is six o'clock and "the master not home yet"; Sabina—the sexy maid who sometimes steps out of her part to complain about the play—is parodying the chitchat that often opens a realistic well-made

1. Mary McCarthy, *"The Skin of Our Teeth,"* in *Sights and Spectacles* (New York: Farrar, Straus and Cudahy, 1956). 2. *The Journals of Thornton Wilder 1939–1961.* Selected and edited by Donald Gallup. (New Haven: Yale University Press, 1985).

play: "If anything happened to him, we would certainly be inconsolable and have to move into a less desirable residential district." The dramatic movement—never Wilder's strong point—involves waiting for Antrobus, contending with the cold, disciplining a dinosaur and a mastodon, receiving Antrobus's messages about surviving ("burn everything except Shakespeare"), and living in a typical bickering American family; Maggie Antrobus—unlike her inventive, intellectual, progressive husband—is instinctual and practical. Her children, Henry and Gladys, are emblems of violence and sexuality: the boy has obviously killed his brother with a stone; the girl has trouble keeping her dress down. When their father arrives home—with a face like that of a Keystone Cop, a tendency to pinch Sabina, and a line of insults that sounds like W.C. Fields, the plot moves a bit more swiftly. He asks the dinosaur to leave and receives Homer and Moses into the house. As the act ends, the family of man is trying to conserve its ideas and knowledge—including the alphabet and arithmetic; it has also accepted "the refugees"—the Greek poet and the Hebrew lawgiver. The fire of civilization is alive, and members of the audience are asked to pass up chairs to keep it going.

Act II has the glitz of Atlantic City and the continuing problem of Mr. Antrobus dealing with the disasters of terrestrial life, the fact of his own sexuality, and the gnawing obligations of a father and husband. Once again, in the style of Brecht's epic theater, an announcer comments on screen projections—"Fun at the Beach" and the events of the convocation of "the Ancient and Honorable Order of Mammals." The plot is jumpier than ever—Miss Lily Sabina Fairweather, Miss Atlantic City 1942, tries to seduce Antrobus; a fortune-teller squawks about coming rains; Mrs. Antrobus bickers with the children, champions the idea of the family, and protests against Antrobus's breaking of his marriage promise; Antrobus, ashamed of himself at last, shepherds his flock and an assortment of animals into a boat.

THE INEVITABLE BUSINESS OF ENDURING

Dealing with the effects of war, Act III is a powerful ending to this play about surviving. The wild and often inspired stage gimmickry of the first two acts has given way to the darkened stage and the ravaged Antrobus home. The emotions become more concentrated, the actions and efforts seem less scattered, the people's situations reach us as both tragedy and the inevitable business of men and women enduring. A play that seemed to be in revolt against realistic character representation, psychological probing, and the fine shadings of nineteenth-century drama, explodes into a moving exploration of personalities as they face the modern world. Deeply affected by the suffering of the war, the family members come into focus as human beings rather than emblems. Henry, the linchpin of this act about war and violence, explains himself for the first time and becomes more than a stick figure. Resentful about having "anybody over me" he has turned himself into a fascist as a way of mastering the authorities—his father, especially––who oppressed him. His truculence, fierce selfishness, and horrible individualism make him both a believable neurotic and a distillation of brutal resentment. Sabina, the temptress who has competed with Mrs. Antrobus for the attention of George, also comes alive as an individual. Driven to depression and cynicism by the hardship of the war, she pronounces that people "have a right to grab what they can find." As "just an ordinary girl" who doesn't mind dealing in black-market goods to pay for a night at the movies, she represents Wilder's honest appraisal of what suffering often does to people. Antrobus—the principle of light, reason, and progress in the play—also has his moments of depression. He yearns for simple relief: "Just a desire to settle down; to slip into the old grooves and keep the neighbors from walking over my lawn." But somehow a pile of old tattered books, brought to life by passages from Spinoza, Plato, and Aristotle delivered by stand-in actors, rekindles the desire "to start building." Self-interest, complacency, despair, and violence coexist with intellectual aspirations and energies to begin again: although outnumbered by ordinarily self-involved and extraordinarily violent people, Antrobus can still go on. Despite the fact that the play ends, as it began, with "the world at sixes and sevens," there is still the principle of the family in Mrs. Antrobus's words and the desire to create the future from the past in Mr. Antrobus's reverence for Plato and technology.

A JUMBLE OF DRAMATIC STYLES

The styles of this play are as various as modern literature and the twentieth-century stage. Not at all austere or carefully crafted, the drama is a brilliant jumble of Pirandello, Joyce, and epic theater.

Once again Wilder employs the manner, and the basic outlook, of *Six Characters in Search of an Author*. Sabina and Henry, particularly, make us aware that they are performing, that their parts are not entirely to their liking, and that they want to convey something about themselves that the theater does not have the means to express. Just as Pirandello's actors distort the story of a tragic family, Wilder's script does not always allow Sabina to tell about her truths or Henry to explain his real-life motivations. Like Pirandello's agonized daughter-figure, Henry insists on the brutal truth of his situation and interrupts the flow of the action to cry out against the false representation that he is given by the playwright. The management of the stage business in *The Skin of Our Teeth* is another reminder of Pirandello's theater. The awkward, clumsy matter of props and their arrangement leads us back to *Six Characters* and its arguments about where people should stand, what a room was like, and how people should look. Wilder delights in offering us not only a drama of survival, but also the laborious process of making a play—the scaffolding of a work of art is just as much his subject as the work itself. The stops and starts, the interruptions and localized quarrels of the actors, the puncturing of the whole theatrical illusion by the reality of actors who have become sick from some food and need to be replaced: such ploys carry through Wilder's theme of struggle and endurance, but also suggest the impact of Pirandello's artfully disordered dramas. Wilder's debt to Pirandello does not end with stage technique. The vision of the play—Antrobus beginning again and the family ready "to go on for ages and ages yet"—has most often been traced to Joyce's *Finnegans Wake:* Wilder himself acknowledged this partial debt in the midst of the brouhaha about his "plagiarism." Other influences were overlooked. Pirandello's tragic and tormented family in *Six Characters* goes offstage only to find another theater in which to play out its drama: in a mood of guarded optimism, this is precisely what the Antrobus family is about to do. Sabina reports that they are on their way.

The Skin of Our Teeth also becomes a more enjoyable and intelligible theatrical experience when it is placed beside Bertolt Brecht's epic-theater works. The staging, character presentation, themes, and generalizing power bear an important relationship to Brecht's experiments in the

1930s.³ Without having to argue for direct influences, one still can see a great deal about Wilder's techniques and idea by placing them in apposition to a work like *Mother Courage.* Since both plays take place in time of war, employ epic exaggeration, explore violence and selfishness, and take an unadorned look at what suffering does to people, it is not unreasonable to view them together. *Mother Courage* was also written three years before *The Skin of Our Teeth,* a fact that is not without significance considering Wilder's close touch with the currents of twentieth-century literature. Yet whether he was influenced directly or not, the affinities are strong. As pieces of stagecraft, both plays employ a large historical sweep and present material in a nonrealistic manner; Brecht's play of the Thirty Years War and Wilder's play of civilization's disaster both reach for large generalizations about man's durability and defects. The works do this essentially didactic job by means of screen projections, announcers, jagged episodic plots, and characters who are often stereotypical or emblematic. Wilder's third act overcomes Brecht's relentless detachment from his characters, but even here—as we sympathize with Sabina and Henry—we are not in a theater where the individual psyche is the main concern. Wilder is more involved with the process of learning, the hope of progress, and the impediments in human nature and culture than with the individuality of his people. In this he is one with Brecht, a writer who studies the harshness of civilization and the brutality of ordinary folk. Sabina's selfish, compromising, essentially amoral view of the human struggle for survival is like nothing so much as Mother Courage's matter-of-fact attitude toward suffering and willingness to hitch up her wagon and do business after her children are dead. Wilder has humanized and intellectualized this savage world, but he essentially works with its terrifying ingredients. Even Antrobus, the beacon light of the three acts, is tainted by the lust, a cynicism, cheapness, and hypocrisy that Brecht saw as the central features of bourgeois life. While Antrobus brings his noble and selfish impulses into a unity, he is still like Humanity as described by Brecht in *Saint Joan of the Stockyards:*

3. See also Douglas Wixon, Jr., "The Dramatic Techniques of Thornton Wilder and Bertolt Brecht," *Modern Drama,* XV, no. 2 (September 1972). This informative essay gives special attention to the anti-illusionist theater of Brecht and Wilder; it argues that Wilder employed Brechtian techniques from 1931 onward. The article does not explore the thematic affinities of the two writers.

Humanity! Two souls abide
Within thy breast!
Do not set either one aside:
To live with both is best!
Be torn apart with constant care!
Be two in one! Be here, be there!
Hold the low one, hold the high one—
Hold the straight one, hold the sly one—
Hold the pair![4]

During the period when Wilder was working on *The Skin of Our Teeth,* the influence of *Finnegans Wake* was also taking effect on his vision. In his correspondence with Edmund Wilson in 1940 and 1941 Wilder gave his own version of the Joyce connection and offered a perspective on his imagination that is more wide-ranging than Robinson and Campbell's detective work. Wilder explained to Wilson that the *Wake* was a book with "a figure in the carpet": the design, he argued, was to be discovered in Joyce's anal eroticism; the great conundrum of modern literature was all about "order, neatness, single-minded economy of means."[5] Whether or not this is a reductive interpretation of Joyce, the "discovery" tells us something about Wilder's mind, points to his own career as a preserver of other people's motifs, and suggests a possible explanation for his constant borrowings in *The Skin.* Wilder claimed that he felt a joyous "relief"[6] as he understood Joyce's psychic and literary strategies; each interpreter of these remarks (and of Wilder's *Wake* obsessions) will have to decide what they are revealing. But the present study of Wilder's imagination offers this material as another example of his loving accumulation of ideas and patterns. The letters are a way of coming to terms with his own nature.

Writing to Wilson, Wilder spoke of the *Wake* as embodying "the neurotic's frenzy to tell and not tell."[7] Tell what? the reader might ask. Once again, this remark might be turned on Wilder's own work-in-progress: there are at least two of Wilder's recurring anxieties in the new play—resentment and guilt felt by a son *and* fear of civilization's destruction. His play, Wilder told Wilson, was meant to dramatize "the end of the world in comic strip."[8] On one level the description matched Joyce's remarks that *Finnegans Wake* is "a farce of destiny." But Wilder's readers cannot help recalling

4. *Seven Plays* (Brecht), ed. Eric Bentley (New York: Grove Press, 1961). 5. Letter to Edmund Wilson (January 13, 1940), Beinecke Library. 6. Letter to Edmund Wilson (June 15, 1940), Beinecke Library. 7. Ibid. 8. Letter to Edmund Wilson (June 26, 1940), Beinecke Library.

the disaster of *The Bridge*, the end of the patrician world in *The Cabala*, the declining pagan world in *The Woman of Andros*. *The Skin of Our Teeth* may be seen as both a Joyce-burdened work and the latest version of Wilder's anxieties about violence and the collapse of Western culture.

The folk-style of *Our Town*, the social parable of *The Merchant of Yonkers*, and the rich suggestiveness and borrowing of *The Skin of Our Teeth* are three forms of expression that Wilder developed to convey the struggle of people enduring the churnings of the cosmos and the conflicts of civilization. The three plays offer guarded affirmations about man's strivings: growth and insight are abundantly available in Wilder's theater and make it altogether unlike the visions of other major American playwrights.

Chronology

1897

Thornton Niven Wilder is born in Madison, Wisconsin, on April 17. His identical twin dies within a few hours of birth.

1906–1911

Father, Amos P. Wilder, is appointed American consul general to Hong Kong; the family accompanies him to his new post, where Thornton attends a German school. After only six months, Isabella Wilder, Thornton's mother, takes the children to Berkeley, California, where they reside until 1911.

1911

The family rejoins their father in Shanghai, where he is now posted. After a short stint at another German school, Thornton attends the China Inland Mission Boys and Girls School at Chefoo.

1912–1915

Back in California, Thornton attends school in Ojai and Berkeley, graduating from Berkeley High School in 1915.

1914–1918

World War I; the United States enters the war in 1917.

1915–1917

Wilder attends Oberlin College in Ohio; some of his earliest works are published in the *Oberlin Literary Magazine*.

1917

Transfers to Yale University in New Haven, Connecticut.

1918

Yale Literary Magazine publishes several of his short plays and essays.

1918–1919

After a summer working for the War Industries Board in Washington, D.C., tries to enlist, but several armed services reject him for poor eyesight. Accepted by the Coast Artillery Corps, he serves for a few months as a corporal in Rhode Island, after which he returns to Yale.

1920

After serving for a year on the editorial board of the *Yale Literary Magazine* (which publishes his play *The Trumpet Shall Sound* as a serial), he graduates with a bachelor of arts degree. F. Scott Fitzgerald publishes *This Side of Paradise;* Sinclair Lewis publishes *Main Street;* Nineteenth Amendment grants women the right to vote.

1920–1921

In Rome, at the American Academy, Wilder studies archeology and begins writing *The Cabala*. After a year abroad, he returns to the United States to teach French at Lawrenceville, a boys' school in New Jersey.

1922

Fitzgerald publishes *The Beautiful and Damned;* James Joyce publishes *Ulysses;* T.S. Eliot publishes *The Waste Land.*

1924

Takes a leave of absence to attend graduate school at Princeton University.

1925

Receives M.A. in French literature from Princeton; spends the summer at MacDowell Colony in New Hampshire. Begins writing *The Bridge of San Luis Rey*, continuing to work on it in Europe that fall. Fitzgerald publishes *The Great Gatsby.*

1926

The Cabala is published. Ernest Hemingway publishes *The Sun Also Rises.*

1927

Wilder returns to Lawrenceville; *The Bridge of San Luis Rey* is published.

1928

Receives Pulitzer Prize for *The Bridge of San Luis Rey.* Publishes *The Angel That Troubled the Waters.* Resigns from Lawrenceville and goes to Europe, where he works on *The Woman of Andros.*

1929

William Faulkner publishes *The Sound and the Fury.*

1929–1937

Great Depression follows the stock market crash of October 29, 1929.

1930

Wilder publishes *The Woman of Andros.* Begins lecturing in comparative literature at the University of Chicago.

1931

Publishes *The Long Christmas Dinner and Other Plays.*

1933

President Franklin Roosevelt introduces his New Deal, programs intended to end the depression.

1935

Wilder meets Gertrude Stein, beginning a long, warm friendship. Publishes *Heaven's My Destination.* Italy invades Ethiopia.

1936–1939

Spanish Civil War.

1937

Japan invades China.

1938

Germany annexes Austria. *Our Town* opens in New York, receives Pulitzer Prize. *The Merchant of Yonkers* opens in New York.

1939

John Steinbeck publishes *The Grapes of Wrath.*

1939–1945

World War II. The United States enters the war in 1941, after the December 7 Japanese attack on Pearl Harbor.

1942

Wilder writes movie script *The Shadow of a Doubt* for Alfred Hitchcock. Enlists in the air force, where he is commissioned a captain. *The Skin of Our Teeth* opens in New York.

1942–1943

Serves in Africa. Receives his third Pulitzer Prize in 1943 for *The Skin of Our Teeth.*

1945

Leaves the air force in September.

1948

Publishes *The Ides of March.*

1950–1951

Awarded the Charles Eliot Norton Professorship of Poetry at Harvard University, where he lectures on "The American Characteristics in Classic American Literature."

1952

American Academy of Arts and Letters awards him its gold medal for fiction.

1963

Awarded the Presidential Medal of Freedom.

1964

Hello, Dolly!, based on *The Matchmaker,* first produced for the stage.

1965

Awarded the National Medal of Literature.

1967

Publishes *The Eighth Day.*

1968

Awarded the National Book Award for *The Eighth Day*.

1973

Publishes *Theophilus North*.

1975

Thornton Wilder dies December 7.

FOR FURTHER RESEARCH

Martin Blank, ed., *Critical Essays on Thornton Wilder.* New York: G.K. Hall, 1996.

Jackson R. Bryer, ed., *Conversations with Thornton Wilder.* Jackson: University Press of Mississippi, 1992.

Edward Burns, Ulla E. Dydo, and William Rice, eds., *The Letters of Gertrude Stein and Thornton Wilder.* New Haven, CT: Yale University Press, 1996.

David Castronovo, *Thornton Wilder.* New York: Ungar, 1986.

Malcolm Goldstein, *The Art of Thornton Wilder.* Omaha: University of Nebraska Press, 1965.

Richard H. Goldstone, *Thornton Wilder: An Intimate Portrait.* New York: Saturday Review Press, 1975.

Richard H. Goldstone and Gary Anderson, *Thornton Wilder. An Annotated Bibliography of Works by and About Thornton Wilder.* New York: AMS Press, 1982.

Bernard Grebanier, *Thornton Wilder.* Minneapolis: University of Minnesota Press, 1964.

Donald Haberman, *The Plays of Thornton Wilder.* Middletown, CT: Wesleyan University Press, 1967.

Gilbert A. Harrison, *The Enthusiast: A Life of Thornton Wilder.* New Haven, CT: Ticknor & Fields, 1983.

M.C. Kuner, *Thornton Wilder: The Bright and the Dark.* New York: Crowell, 1972.

Paul Lifton, *Vast Encyclopedia: The Theatre of Thornton Wilder.* Westport, CT: Greenwood Press, 1995.

Elizabeth Barron McCasland, *The Philosophy of Thornton Wilder.* New York: Carlton Press, 1976.

Helmut Papajewski, *Thornton Wilder.* Trans. John Conway. New York: Ungar, 1968.

Linda Simon, *Thornton Wilder: His World.* Garden City, NY: Doubleday, 1979.

Amos Niven Wilder, *Thornton Wilder and His Public.* Philadelphia: Fortress Press, 1980.

Mary Ellen Williams (Walsh), *A Vast Landscape: Time in the Novels of Thornton Wilder.* Pocatello: Idaho State University Press, 1979.

THE WORLD WIDE WEB

There are a variety of Wilder resources on the Internet; the editors direct interested readers to a website being developed by the Columbia University Graduate School of the Arts, in honor of Wilder's centenary, as a promising starting point for research. Find the website at **www.columbia.edu/cu/arts/wilder/index.html.** Its "wilder.net" link on the Education Resources page claims it will link to "every on-line resource with a connection to Thornton Wilder."

WORKS BY THORNTON WILDER

NOVELS

The Cabala (1926)

The Bridge of San Luis Rey (1927)

The Woman of Andros (1930)

Heaven's My Destination (1935)

The Ides of March (1948)

The Eighth Day (1967)

Theophilus North (1973)

PLAYS

Our Town (1938)

The Merchant of Yonkers (1939)

The Skin of Our Teeth (1942)

The Matchmaker (1955)

The Alcestiad (1955)

The Drunken Sisters (1957), (a satyr play, published with *The Alcestiad)*

COLLECTIONS OF SHORT PLAYS

The Angel That Troubled the Waters and Other Plays (1928)

The Long Christmas Dinner and Other Plays (1931)

ESSAYS

"Some Thoughts on Playwriting," in *The Intent of the Artist*, edited by Augusto Cereno (1941)

American Characteristics and Other Essays (1979) (published posthumously)

JOURNALS

The Journals of Thornton Wilder, 1939–1961. (1985) Selected and edited by Donald Gallup, with two scenes of an uncompleted play, *The Emporium* (published posthumously)

INDEX